MEETING FAMOUS CHRISTIANS

by
Brian G. Cooper

MAYHEW-McCRIMMON

Great Wakering

First published in Great Britain in 1977 by
MAYHEW-McCRIMMON LTD
Great Wakering Essex England

© Copyright 1977 by Brian G. Cooper

ISBN 0 85597 205 X

Cover design: Russell North.

Contents

The author thanks the editors of *Baptist Times* and *Christian Weekly Newspapers* for permission to use material originally published in article form in these journals.

To Wendy

Introduction

In these pages, I have tried to let twelve outstanding Christians speak for themselves. I hope that through Meeting Famous Christians, your own Christian life and experience will be enriched by their achievement and vision as mine have been.

The twelve Christian men and women we encounter in this book are regarded as outstanding examples of the Christian faith in life and action today. They come from different denominational traditions and theological streams — Anglican, Catholic, Church of Scotland, Evangelical, Free Church, Orthodox — yet they have much in common. All live very close to God and very close to their fellow men and women. All are motivated by a Christ-centred worldliness. All have made their Christianity utterly relevant to the problem-ridden secular world of the late twentieth century. All are powerful communicators, with an infectious enthusiasm for the things of the Gospel and Kingdom. To be with them is to encounter those for whom God is utterly for real in both His Church and His world.

Between them, they encompass what is to me central to the faithfulness of Christian witness and the credibility of the Gospel in our time: the renewal of prayer, spirituality and the inner life of the Church, and the engagement of the Church with the critical issues of today's world — especially racial equality, justice for the poor and peace built on true community and the fellowship of the whole human family.

The appeal of these outstanding Christians is international. They have already had a considerable influence within the British Churches; I hope that this book will contribute towards their wider influence.

To those inside the Church who say despairingly "Where are the great Christians of our day?", I would point to them as examples. But this book would fail if it merely produced a religious hero worship. Its purpose is to inspire to Christian commitment and action for God's Kingdom and His world today.

Brian G. Cooper.

The publisher wishes to thank the following for permission to use their copyright photographs:

Thames Television for the photograph of Metropolitan Bloom.

John Pridmore for the photograph of Archbishop Camara.

Universal Pictorial Press, London for the photo of Bishop Huddleston, of Brother Schutz and of Bishop Winter.

Church of Scotland Publicity Office for the photo of Lord MacLeod.

The Press Association for the photo of Bishop Sheppard and of Sheila Cassidy.

Scoop Press Agency for the photo of Cardinal Suenens.

Syndication International photo division (Daily Mirror) for the photo of Sally Trench.

Methodist Missionary Society for the photo of Pauline Webb.

Bill Doyle of Dublin for the photo of Michel Quoist.

Life in the Spirit

Metropolitan Anthony Bloom

Metropolitan Anthony Bloom
Life in the Spirit

The most popular religious leader on your television screen represents a denomination with less than two thousand followers in Britain. To the vast majority of viewers, whether or not they are Christian, his tradition of churchmanship is mysterious and remote — perhaps even slightly exotic. His appeal is, in many ways, surprising. He learned English quite late in life. Most of his life he has spent outside Britain. No high-pressure evangelistic organisation backs him. Yet when he speaks on TV or radio, many among the vast public of non-churchgoers stop and listen — and take notice. "This man is different", they say. He speaks very simply, rarely using long words, and never indulging in flights of oratory. Yet he projects a profound spirituality, and an enormous sense of the depths of life in God.

When Archbishop Anthony Bloom starts talking, you know God is for real.

One of the most remarkable Christians of our century, Archbishop Anthony is a very eminent and highly respected figure of the Russian Orthodox Church. For eleven years until Easter 1974, as senior Orthodox prelate in Western Europe, and representative in the West of Patriarch Pimen of Moscow, he travelled frequently across the continent, visiting and advising Orthodox priests and people from Amsterdam to Morocco, and from Stockholm to Brussels. Responsibility for inter-Church contacts has meant frequent visits to the Vatican and to the World Council of Churches' headquarters in Geneva. Regular visits to the Soviet Union to meet its Church leaders and teach its theological academies, feature in his programme.

"My ikon is my passport", he once joked to me, referring to the bejewelled religious miniature he wears on his cassock.

Yet it is as a man of spiritual power, and strong living prayer, that we think of him, not as a jet-setting ecclesiastic. From TV screen, pulpit or platform, his obvious holiness of life and closeness to God, come across to all. His broadcasts and writings on prayer reach a vast and eager audience, comprising Christians of every denomination and shade of churchmanship — and non-Christians, fascinated by the man and the reality of his life with God. When Archbishop Anthony talks about the Holy Spirit, as he frequently does, any lingering doubts that the Holy Spirit is alive and well and at work in our world of today, are soon dispelled. The thousands of letters he receives testify that many people inside and outside the Church gain new life in God through his rich ministry — "a single broadcast can lead to hundreds of letters. It leads to a lot of extra work! But it is a special and personal way of reaching people".

Certainly Anthony Bloom, who now has pastoral oversight for the fifteen hundred Russian Orthodox Christians scattered throughout the British Isles, is among the most remarkable people I have ever met. Indeed, almost everything about him is remarkable — his early life, his conversion to the Christian Faith, how he came to England, his tireless travelling. Also a source of wonder to me is the sheer fact that he packs so much into a single day yet never seems rushed. His immensely varied experience of life, and his genius in reflecting spiritually upon his own life and the world generally, make him a man in demand for counselling those in need of God's guidance. His insight into others is quick and profound. Many have turned a completely new chapter in life, after talking with Archbishop Anthony.

His story begins in 1914, the year of the outbreak of the First World War. He was born the son of a high-ranking Russian diplomat serving the Czar on a special international mission in Lausanne, Switzerland. It was three years before the Russian Revolution. The coming of war saw the family move to Persia. The young Anthony had begun his amazing life of adventure, travel and challenge, in many ways unique. For it was also to prove a very unusual spiritual odyssey, too. The way of spiritual searching and religious pilgrimage that led the diplomat's son eventually to become Russian Orthodox Metropolitan of Western Europe — and simply 'Metropolitan Anthony' to millions — was a unique adventure into Faith.

So what happened to the small boy in Persia during the First World War?

"The Russian Revolution came, and my father had to leave the diplomatic service. We were in northern Persia at the time. I remember it as a vastness, arid and burnt. I was seven before I saw a car, eight before I knew electric light. We sailed down the Tigris and Euphrates on a barge — I recall going through 'the Garden of Eden'. Then we travelled from Basra to India, from where we sailed on an English ship to Gibraltar. Then to Spain, across Europe to Austria, where I was sent to school, and so on to Paris, to complete my schooling and then go to university."

Settling in Paris, he qualified as a doctor, a calling he followed, as a physician and surgeon in Paris, in the French Army and French Resistance during the war against Hitler, and then again in peacetime, until finally becoming a priest early in 1949.

I use the word 'calling' deliberately: Anthony Bloom's decision to be a physician followed directly upon his remarkable conversion to the Living Christ. How did that happen? Suprisingly, his contact with religion of any kind was very limited until well into his teens.

"I didn't come from a devout Orthodox background. I don't remember being in churches as a child. It wasn't an anti-religious atmosphere, but my father was very interested in the Eastern religions, rather than Christianity. Of course, I had been baptised into Orthodox Christianity, but it wasn't a real thing for me in the early part of my life. I became a convert to the Orthodoxy into which I had been baptised, when I was fifteen, while studying science to go to medical school."

One day, invited to a talk on Christianity being given by an Orthodox priest, the young Anthony Bloom sat through it 'very unwillingly!' Then he went home, and decided to check what he had heard, with the Gospel narrative. Not wanting to spend too long over it, he chose the shortest Gospel — St. Mark's.

The few moments that followed changed the whole course of his life.

"I met Christ as a person at a moment when I needed him in order to live — and yet at a moment when I was not in search of him. I was found — I did not find him. It happened like this. While reading the Gospel I became aware of a presence. I saw nothing. I heard nothing. It was no hallucination. It was a simple certainty that the Lord was standing there and that I was in the presence of him whose life I had begun to read with such revulsion and ill-will. From then I knew that Christ did exist, that he was the Risen Christ. The impossible event of the Resurrection was to me more certain than any event of history."

It was the moment of his conversion — and the moment of his calling soon followed.

"When I discovered what the Gospel meant, I decided life could not be lived apart from that, and I would become a physician, serve among the poor, and eventually be ordained."

For fifteen years, in war and peace, Anthony Bloom worked as a devoted physician in his adopted country, France. The years of the Second World War, when France was occupied by Nazi Germany, saw him in the Resistance movement — his was no otherworldly faith! He comments on those dangerous days: "I felt I had to join the Resistance struggle. I was convinced that Nazism must not spread, and I wanted to live in solidarity with the French people. But I remained passionately Russian, in my love of the Russian language, literature and history!"

He did not expect to leave his adopted country. God had other plans. In the post-1945 years, the Fellowship of St. Alban and St. Sergius, an organisation for promoting links and understanding between the Church of England and the Orthodox Churches, invited him to England to give lectures on the Orthodox Church. After a number of such visits, he was invited to become Orthodox chaplain to the Fellowship in 1949, and accepted. So he came to live and work in England. Possessing a considerable flair for languages, he soon mastered English!

Already, in 1943, while still a physician, he had professed monastic vows; he was ordained to the priesthood five years later. Over the years the Russian Orthodox Church gave him more and more responsibilities. In 1950, he was appointed Vicar of the Russian Patriarchal Parish in London, and was consecrated Bishop eight years later. He was made Archbishop in charge of the Russian Orthodox Church in Great Britain in 1962, subsequently becoming also Orthodox Metropolitan of the whole of Western Europe. A member of the Orthodox Holy Synod, he became a regular visitor to the Church in the Soviet Union, and did much to represent the Orthodox Church in the worldwide movement for closer understanding and unity of all Christians, the Ecumenical Movement. Yet it is not as a church official that Archbishop Bloom has become such a much-respected and much-loved leader and inspirer of Christians — but as a man of great spiritual insight and real pastoral concern.

He tells of his activities and delight in working among the young. "I travel a lot, meeting priests and believers, both singly and in groups. Lecturing occupies a great deal of my time, too, especially at theological colleges, schools, universities and conferences. I most enjoy talking to students, and being with ordinands on retreats, explaining about Prayer, or about Orthodoxy generally. Orthodoxy has come on the religious map in recent years, and students particularly want to know its message. I must help to meet their spiritual search."

For countless thousands outside his own Orthodox tradition, Anthony Bloom has been guide and inspiration into a real, personal knowledge of God. Yet he never neglects his own flock: "I am diocesan bishop of all Orthodox Christians throughout Britain and Ireland, and must supervise their needs — and that means even more travelling!"

Working long hours each day, and covering many thousands of miles each year, Archbishop Bloom's busy schedule would daunt the most energetic jet-set executive! No wonder he is a familiar figure to airport officials all over Europe! His efforts remain untiring, in spite of bouts of ill-health.

Many people in this day and age find prayer very difficult. Even to many inside the Christian Church, prayer often seems unreal — though most would not admit it. Yet more and more people want to pray in a fashion they find meaningful. Archbishop Anthony has done more than most Church leaders in our time to make prayer come alive again. From the ancient and rich spiritual tradition of the Orthodox Church, he speaks about prayer with authority and depth, yet with simplicity. His 'Schools for Prayer' draw a wide following from people of all ages and religious backgrounds. His books on prayer are best sellers. Young people flock to hear him unfold the mystery of prayer, in the language they can understand — yet Archbishop Anthony uses no gimmicks. A prayerful attitude permeating the whole of one's life, rather than special techniques or systems of spiritual exercises, is what counts, he stresses.

"A sense of rapport with God is the proper criterion of a prayerful attitude. That is what it means to be 'in the mind of Christ.' Prayer is relationship to God. No one can teach you to pray any more than you can be taught to relate to someone. Stand in God's presence, simple, open, and ready to work with him — that is the way of prayer." Real Christian action must be rooted in prayer — "Christian action should be defined as an action of God mediated through a person. There is no such Christianity without a sustained contemplative attitude."

Archbishop Anthony Bloom once put it this way in a radio interview: "When you think of Christ you see him continuously listening to the depths of the divine silence that contains the wisdom and the love of God, and thinking out what it is. You can see him watching God's work and articulating it — and this is what I believe to be the Christian vocation in both contemplation and activity."

Certainly the Archbishop's own life proves that even in this busy modern age, we can 'be still and know God' while living each day to the full. He emphasises that every day is given by God to us to be given back to Him — and for Anthony Bloom, a typical day includes not only travelling, speaking, writing and conducting prayer and worship, but also being available to people. He may spend anything up to ten hours in a single day giving spiritual guidance to those who come seeking counsel on how to deepen their spiritual lives. He told me he tries not to turn any seeker away: "I try not to refuse to see people. But I won't be their spiritual mentor on a regular basis if they belong to another tradition; that's not fair."

Until very recently, the Orthodox tradition in Christianity was unfamiliar, indeed virtually unknown, to most Christians in Britain. Archbishop Anthony Bloom, almost single-handed, has opened its treasures to many — especially its rich yet simple insights into the spiritual way, and the life of prayer. All this is summed-up in his challenge to "Live in the Holy Spirit!", one of his favourite themes. I shall always remember the early hours of one morning, during a great all-night vigil in one of our most historic cathedrals, when Archbishop Anthony gave this challenge to hundreds of young people, gathered for several hours of prayer, worship and meditation.

"The Holy spirit is always a dynamic of life and joy, leading things from what they are to what they are called to be, brooding forever over the chaos to bring order and beauty out of it. So our vocation is to live in the Spirit — not to be more and more remarkable animals, but to be the sons and companions of God in eternity."

Archbishop Anthony Bloom challenges and inspires Christians everywhere to live in the Holy Spirit.

Archbishop Anthony Bloom: Key facts
Born in 1914 in Switzerland, son of Russian diplomat. Educated in Paris. 1929: conversion experience. Trained as doctor; served as physician and surgeon in France until becoming priest in 1949. Served in French Army and Resistance in Second World War. 1943: took monastic vows. 1949: became an Orthodox priest. 1949: came to Britain to be chaplain to the Fellowship of St. Alban and St. Sergius. 1950: appointed vicar of the Russian Patriarchal Parish in London. 1958: consecrated bishop. 1962: appointed Archbishop in charge of the Russian Orthodox Church in Great Britain and Ireland. 1963: appointed Exarch of Western Europe to the Patriarch of Moscow. 1966-74: Orthodox Metropolitan of Western Europe. Retains pastoral oversight of Orthodoxy in Britain. *Books include: School for Prayer* and contribution to: *We Believe in God*

Prophet of the Poor

Archbishop Helder Camara

Archbishop Helder Camara

Prophet of the Poor

Military coups and threats of revolution, torture and denial of human rights, kidnappings by urban guerillas — all mean that Latin America is rarely far from the headlines. In that continent with such great extremes of wealth and poverty, the most passionate advocate of social justice is no guerilla, general or Marxist hero, but a remarkable Christian leader. Dom Helder Camara is a Roman Catholic prelate, the Archbishop of Olinda and Recife in north-east Brazil. For many millions in his own country and throughout Latin America, and indeed across the globe, he is the 'voice of the voiceless,' the spokesman of the poor and oppressed.

His fearless advocacy of social and economic justice, in the name of the liberating power of Christ, is now known world-wide. Undoubtedly, he is among the most famous Roman Catholic churchmen today, and certainly one of the most significant Christian prophets of our time. This is acknowledged by many outside the Church: in 1975 he was awarded the World Humanity Award in London, by Lord Mountbatten. He has been nominated several times for the Nobel Peace Prize. Small of physical stature, yet immense in his courage and compassion, Helder Camara seeks no self-publicity — his personality absolutely radiates humility — but only the opportunity to relate the Gospel to our world, torn by the extremes of wealth and poverty.

To meet him is at once to be aware of being in the presence of a man of enormous moral strength and spiritual power. In private conversation he is quiet, almost self-effacing. On the public platform, his oratory is powerful, his advocacy of the cause of the world's poor vehement. Kindly, with an unmistakeable sparkle in his eyes, and with a rare combination of gentleness and strength, in private and public alike, the sheer magnetism of his personality comes across unforgettably.

Quite simply, his spirituality and zeal for social righteousness are truly Christ-like. Of course, this should not surprise us! His concern for the poor, and his stern denunciations of both the evils under which they suffer, and the groups and nations responsible for those evils, derive directly from the Gospel of Christ.

"The Church's commission is to take seriously a religion committed to the liberation of man, not only after death throughout a long and mysterious eternity but also during this life here on earth."

The Gospel for eternal life and for this life means Christ's liberation of man from selfishness, the basic cause of so much evil on our world.

"It is quite possible to care about eternal life and also give counsel about what happens on earth — but for the love of God, as a work of mercy, and never in terms of law. Christ came to free us from sin and the consequences of sin, from selfishness and the results of selfishness." Helder Camara stresses that this means liberating people from the effects of the selfishness of others — effects very obvious in the poverty-stricken regions of the Third World, such as his native Brazil.

Camara's analysis is uncomfortable and challenging: the peoples of the Third World, and particularly of Latin America, are trapped in an unjust system of business and trade, which benefits only the few, and is organised for the profit of rich elites and outside commercial interests. He sees today's world as Christ's parable of the rich man and the beggar, writ large: the poor of the earth are Lazarus plundered by the Dives of the rich nations of Europe and North America. The latter's big business corporations and multi-national companies use their trade and investment to uphold profiteering and hold back the self-development of the local people. They take out of the Third World countries far more in dividends than is ever ploughed back into the health, welfare and education of those countries. Dom Helder sums it up as "a system of corporate sin at the expense of millions made in the divine image, yet denied all hope of fulness of life."

"The system is not only appallingly unjust, but also deeply violent. Malnutrition, disease and grinding poverty make up the daily lot of millions in many lands. Repressive political systems use terror and violence to keep themselves in power, denying basic human rights and freedoms. Technology, given by God as a means towards human fulfilment and creativity, is being misused for human exploitation, violence and estrangement."

Yet Archbishop Camara is neither politician nor economist. Born sixty-eight years ago at the seaport of Fortaleza in north-east Brazil, as an older teenager he went into a Roman Catholic seminary to train for the priesthood, and has spent his entire life serving the Roman Catholic Church in his own land and throughout the world.

He became a priest in 1931, devoted much time to helping the poor in the slums of his native state of Ceara, and developed a flair for education. He became Secretary for Education in Ceara, and when he moved to Rio de Janeiro in 1936, continued his educational work, by

1964 becoming a member of the Supreme Council for Education. Contact with the poor of Brazil made him more aware of their plight than many of his fellow churchmen, and he devoted himself to alerting the Catholic Church in Brazil to its social responsibilities. He helped to set up the Conference of Brazilian Bishops, and for twelve years was its General Secretary. In 1955, when he became an auxiliary bishop, he helped found the Latin American Episcopal Council.

Within Brazil itself, he began to tackle the plight of the poor living in squalid conditions in the shanty towns — *favelas* — around Rio. His efforts on their behalf revealed how little the government had done, and when in 1964 Dom Helder was made Archbishop of the ancient see of Olinda and Recife, in the north-east, far from Rio, many saw it as an attempt to remove him from public attention and controversy.

It was not to be. For 1964 was also the year when the military seized power in Brazil, setting up a dictatorship, abolishing civil and democratic liberties, and installing a police state to silence all criticism. The education and land reform programmes which Dom Helder and the Conference of Catholic Bishops had helped develop, to improve the lot of the poor, were suppressed. Thousands of people, such as peasant leaders and students, active in these programmes, were put in prison.

The Church was the only organisation left to help the peasants.

It has not been spared terror and oppression. Hundreds of Catholic priests have been imprisoned, many tortured, for seeking to work for the poor. One of Camara's assistants was brutally murdered. On many occasions, the Archbishop's own life has been threatened. His residence has been machine-gunned. For his 'crusade for the poor', for 'peace through justice', makes him very unpopular indeed with Brazil's military dictators. He is not allowed to broadcast on radio or TV. He cannot write articles for Brazil's newspapers. The media are permitted only to mention him if they denounce him. Special anti-Camara TV programmes have even been shown.

The result is that thousands flock to hear his sermons. Notes of what he says are passed from hand to hand. Unwilling to spark off a conflict with the Pope, and thus arouse a hostile reaction throughout the Roman Catholic Church world-wide, the Brazilian government has not dared to silence Archbishop Camara's pulpit declarations. Yet it is a situation fraught with danger, as he uses his position to be 'the voice of the voiceless' in his own land, and on his travels abroad.

In 1969 Archbishop Camara came to Britain to address a big-scale conference of the Student Christian Movement. On subsequent visits, he has addressed Roman Catholic and ecumenical rallies in Liverpool, London and elsewhere. In the tradition of a mediaeval friar, he denounces capitalism as being "fundamentally anti-Christian, having profit as its main concern and highest law." The sin and selfishness of the few, those who direct international investments and trade, causes millions to suffer, frustrating God's purposes for the fulness of life of all His children. The era of political colonialism is passed, but that of economic colonialism is in full swing. Within Latin America and many Third World nations, the very poverty-stricken conditions of life comprise a 'structure of violence.' The child coughing out its tubercular death-agonies in a Recife slum-shack of cardboard and tins, is the living and dying evidence of this institutionalised violence, "the oppressive social structures reducing God's children to sub-human conditions."

"Brethren, these things ought not to be!" he declares to the world.

Change must be motivated by the compassion of Christ. The brave south American archbishop is no Castro-style revolutionary. Utterly opposed to violence in all its forms, Dom Helder fears it will engulf mankind unless justice comes soon. To achieve God's purpose of saving the world from its own sinfulness, the Church must proclaim the Gospel of God's peace through justice among men.

"The Churches should marshall all the moral force they can still command in an attempt to end the manipulation of man, and even if they run the risk of moving out of the religious field, denounce injustices from whatever system they arise, knowing that without justice there will be no peace."

While lashing with righteous anger — and detailed statistics — big American companies which draw back annual profits greater than the entire gross national product of the Latin American country in which they are operating, Archbishop Camara nonetheless has no love of Communism.

"Russia and China impose dialectical materialism by force. They adopt a militant atheism. But fear of Communism should never make Christians blind to the need for radical social and economic changes."

"Take care, Christians, my brothers. Beware of invoking the fear of Communism as an excuse for avoiding a change in the structures which confine millions of the sons of God in a sub-human condition." In the global context, the divide between the rich nations of the North and the poor ones of the South is of far greater significance for the future than the East-West divide, Dom Helder stresses.

"Let us overcome, while there is time, the true clash of this century: between North and South, between countries increasingly richer and countries increasingly poorer!"

Dom Helder has a very strong conviction that, if the Church is to commit itself decisively to the cause of the world's poor, it must not itself be a party to their exploitation. He puts this powerfully, and controversially:

"We Christians are shamed when we see that our denominations make investments in business firms, some of which are engaged in the arms industry, and which nearly all are giddily chasing after a prosperity which derives from the exploitation of those countries which supply the raw materials."

"What have we done with the Gospel of Christ? All the denominations have fallen prey to the capitalist machine. With what remnant of moral authority can we demand structural change if our own institutions are linked to the old structures? Where can we find the clarity of vision to see that our religion, pre-occupied with the defence of the present social order and authority, ends up by supporting the structures of oppression? Can we decide to put aside prestige, social position and money, and accept the risks that Christ told us his followers would have to accept, trusting in the Father who feeds the birds of the air and clothes the lilies of the field?"

Thus Helder Camara challenges the church to be truly itself, if it is to make the Gospel come alive for the poor of the world.

The diminutive archbishop-prophet is a non-violent revolutionary in a continent where the violence of poverty and injustice prevails, breeding revolutionary violence, which in turn results in the state violence of terror and repression. He pleads that man should break out of the cycle of violence. He pleads for peaceful, compassionate change, starkly foreseeing that unless the rich share their wealth — within societies, and between nations — violence will overwhelm whole peoples in terrible fashion.

He firmly believes that if the Third World nations are only allowed to develop in peace without outside interference, then such "self-help" will lead to just development, and a much better life for millions across the globe. He wants the rich nations, like Britain, to give aid, but not to dominate by unequal trade. Significantly, Archbishop Camara believes Britain could play a special role in making a more just world. In November 1975, when he received the World Humanity Award at a special public ceremony at St. Martin-in-the-Fields Church, London, he gave a special "Appeal to Britain," in memorable words:

"Britain, you who created the Commonwealth of Nations, give one step forward! Never dream of being an empire again! Without second thoughts, be a sister to the oppressed peoples! Help wage war on misery, injustices, wars. Help the true, profound, educational reform capable of forming men for their neighbours and for God, and contribute to changing the unjust economic and social structures which crush over two-thirds of the sons of God! Be a living example of a country that is determined to build a more just and more humane world!"

In spite of the terrible poverty he sees daily as he walks the streets of Olinda and Recife, or travels across Brazil and elsewhere in the Third World, and although he knows his own life is constantly in danger, Helder Camara is full of hope. In the idealism of many Christian young people throughout the world, he sees great reason for such hope for the future.

"Young people know that a great part of the coloured world lives in sub-human conditions because of injustices of which it is the victim. Give any of them good food, good clothes, good housing, even the minimum conditions of education, health and work, they can go, with love, as far as — even further than — the white man, in intelligence, culture and virtue."

"Young people do not believe that any separation, any discrimination, any injustice should follow because a man's skin is of a different colour — or because he has a different hairstyle. Young people yearn for a world freed from fear. They see the fear of the poor and the fear of the rich. Material and physical under-development lead to moral under-development. When want, hunger, total dependence on the rich and powerful exist, then there is fear — fear of unemployment, of losing their wretched hovels, fear of arrest, of being beaten and killed."

It is for a world freed from such fears, freed from poverty and injustice, that Archbishop Helder Camara crusades. He challenges us in the rich West to take seriously the Gospel demand for the liberation of the whole man. Certainly he believes passionately in the role of the Church, both his own Roman Catholic institution and the wider Christian community of the world Church, as God's instrument for the transformation of mankind. A beacon of hope for the under-privileged in his own nation and throughout the Third World, Camara challenges us to live for them — in the compassion of Christ.

Archbishop Helder Camara: Key facts
Born 1909 at Fortaleza in North-East Brazil. Entered theological seminary in late teens. 1931: entered the priesthood. Became Secretary of State for Education in Ceara. 1936: moved to Rio de Janeiro. 1955: helped to set up the Latin American Episcopal Council. 1964: became member of the Supreme Council for Education. 1964: military coup in Brazil and ending of democracy. 1964: appointed Archbishop of Olinda and Recife in North-East Brazil. 1969: visited Britain to speak at Student Christian Movement Congress in Manchester. 1972: visited Britain to speak in Liverpool and London. 1975: received World Humanity Award in London. *Books inclu   Church and Colonialism, Race against Time, Spiral of Violence.*

Putting Prayer into Action

Bishop Trevor Huddleston

Bishop Trevor Huddleston
Putting Prayer into Action

No British churchman has done more to awaken the national conscience, of Christians and non-Christians alike, to the evils of racialism than Trevor Huddleston. Bishop of Stepney in East London since 1968, he first hit the headlines over a decade earlier for his courageous fight against apartheid in Johannesburg's sweaty slum of Sophiatown. Later, he held his first episcopal office amid the heady excitements and tough challenges of Nyerere's independent Tanzania in the Sixties, as Bishop of the rural diocese of Masasi. He has never sought publicity for its own sake, but has always recognised the value of the news media for the Christian cause. Refuting cynicism that in our secular age a clergyman needs a gimmick or a scandal to gain a hearing, Trevor Huddleston is known to millions of non-churchgoers who can recognise decisive Christian courage, and respect rocklike convictions about the reality of God and His purpose for mankind.

A Christian best-seller (*Naught for Your Comfort*), TV appearances and Trafalgar Square rallies, prophetic denunciations of British arms sales to South Africa and strong calls for respect for family life and against pornography — above all, his relentless opposition to racism in all its squalid forms — have together made Trevor Huddleston one of the most prominent and widely-respected Christian personalities in Britain today.

Born in Bedford in 1913, educated at Lancing School and Christ Church, Oxford, he decided to enter the Anglican priesthood and trained at Wells Theological College in Somerset. Ordained priest in 1937, he worked in a parish at Swindon before deciding to join the monastic order of the Community of the Resurrection at Mirfield in Yorkshire. In 1943, the Community sent him to South Africa, to be Priest-in-charge at the Sophiatown and Orlando Anglican missions, in the Johannesburg diocese. Schooled by the monastic discipline of the Community and nurtured in its deep Anglo-Catholic spirituality, his was certainly no other-worldly Gospel. Believing every man is worthy of human dignity because God himself became a man, Trevor Huddleston could not keep quiet about the indignities and injustices heaped upon millions of dark-skinned human beings in racialist South Africa.

While in Sophiatown, Huddleston did all he could to improve the lot of the poverty-stricken Africans there. He attacked the vicious system of pass laws and defended its victims. He denounced the brutal methods of the South African police. He organised sports and recreational facilities for unemployed young Africans, often tempted to be drawn into crime through joblessness and personal despair. All this brought him into conflict with the South African authorities, but he continued his courageous stand in spite of many threats.

Huddleston was determined to do all he could not only to resist oppression but also positively to raise the whole quality of the lives of the Africans in the townships. Sometimes he did this in spectacularly imaginative fashion. On one occasion he arranged for the world famous violinist Yehudi Menuhin to give a concert at the Sophiatown church, thronged to overflowing for the sublime sound of that master of music. A concert was something utterly new for the Africans of Sophiatown, but Huddleston did not let it stop there: many other concerts and cultural occasions followed, too.

Harsh political realities intervened. The South African authorities had no desire for the Africans to become educated and appreciate culture, nor any wish for the Church to raise them above a servile status. Father Trevor Huddleston was to be but the first of a series of Anglican churchmen who, over two decades, were expelled or forced to withdraw becase they spoke God's word of justice and practised the Gospel of love. In 1961 the Bishop of Johannesburg, Ambrose Reeves, was to be expelled. Other priests, and bishops like Colin Winter of Namibia, were to follow. Huddleston had been the first to raise his voice. . . .

Returning to England for new duties with the Community of the Resurrection in 1956, Trevor Huddleston did not abandon the oppressed people of South Africa. Now he had a world platform. I vividly remember one Sunday evening in Oxford, when he preached to a University Church congregation of students packed to the doors and standing in the aisles. His message of prophetic Christian concern for social justice in South Africa was thenceforth to be sounded from many pulpits. Even more significant was his best seller *Naught for Your Comfort*, one of the most widely-influential Christian books of our time. Personally, I will always recall, as a young Oxford student, having him autograph my newly-purchased copy of this bombshell book.

It is an uncompromising statement, arising from his own tough experience of life in the slums of Johannesburg. Huddleston had known at first hand the deprivations, hardships and injustices of the Black African people, and determined that the world had to be told. His deep Christian conviction that every man, of whatever colour or race, is of infinite value in God's sight, made him not only fight the inhumanities of the apartheid system while in South Africa but also decide to 'tell it as it is' to the widest possible public.

In *Naught for Your Comfort* he foresaw all too accurately, over two decades ago, the current deep divisions between the black and white races in South Africa and elsewhere, resulting from the lack of understanding, justice and compassion. He sees the issue as not only a fight against racial discrimination, but a campaign for the positive benefits he believes the white, Western world can learn from the African peoples. His eight very hard-working and exhilarating years as Bishop of Masasi in Tanzania, before returning to this country in 1968 to become Bishop of Stepney, confirmed Huddleston in his love of Africa. He was involved in the villages and local churches in helping to build the new nation, in very practical and pastoral ways. He started a school for blind children, an agricultural college and a leprosy treatment centre. This experience strengthened what he had once learned as a young monk: that people need to live in a real and caring community, and are fuller persons when that need is met. In bleak contrast to independent Black Africa's vibrant community spirit and co-operative approach to life, Bishop Huddleston finds our own society in Britain today desperately short of true community spirit. He believes we could learn a lot from the African way!

"Africa is in touch with reality, with bread and water and life as it really is, but in this country today all the standards are materialistic. The mass media spread false values and stimulate people to desire the wrong things. I wish more African clergy could come here, and work among our churches and people. They would bring with them the realities of a different part of the world, where community really means something."

He firmly believes that the experience of African Christians will ultimately contribute to the revitalisation of Christianity throughout the world.

"In independent Black Africa, in so many exciting ways African culture is coming more and more into the Church's life, music and worship. The African Church will eventually produce its own theologians, and the world-wide Christian community will benefit from their thinking. In Africa, where the number of Christians has risen from five million to ninety million over the past half century, there is enormous promise for the whole Christian future."

I have met and talked with Bishop Huddleston on a number of occasions and in a variety of places — at student meetings, on anti-racism platforms, at Church conferences on mission and evangelism, and at his home. The latter is in the heart of his Stepney diocese, in traffic-busy, dirty East London's Commercial Road, a restored Georgian house decorated with paintings and sculpture from his beloved Africa. Tall, ascetic-looking, as memorable to meet as to listen to, he always has that unmistakable impression of a tough holiness and a challenging saintliness. Although he is very outspoken on issues of race and community, it would be quite wrong to label him as a 'political bishop.' His stand on these questions derives from his understanding of God's purposes for mankind, not from any narrow political partisanship. Anyway, most of his working life is spent amid the busy routine of diocesan activities. Amid that routine, and all the civic concerns in the Stepney areas — especially housing, education and community relations — he has to find time for the national and international concerns.

Yet Bishop Trevor Huddleston is such a man of action because he is first a man of prayer.

As a member of the Community of the Resurrection, and very much in the Anglo-Catholic tradition within the Church of England, he is a man of rich, deep and highly disciplined spiritual life. Prayer is something intimate and very real for Trevor Huddleston. He is much in demand to conduct retreats and give lectures on the life of prayer, which he stresses is basic for the renewal of the Church's life and witness. Within his diocese, he puts high priority upon encouraging clergy and lay people alike in their spiritual and devotional lives. His involvement in political causes he sees as "putting prayer into action."

For he insists that prayer must be related to real life, otherwise the prayer itself becomes unreal. His most fervent prayer is that a revitalised Church in Britain will, before it is too late, point the people of our nation to a new sense of national moral purpose, and the abandonment of cynicism and materialism. The 'good life' according to the Christian ideal, means loving God and one's fellow men and women — but too many people in our society are pursuing false materialistic goals of money and affluence, Huddleston observes.

"People respect and respond to a Gospel that asks something of them. The Church should not always be trying to be relevant if in so doing it misses the Gospel. The young want to be challenged by something sacrificial. They are rejecting phoney values and standards. The only hope is to create a community that doesn't live by false values."

As Bishop of Stepney, he has been — and still is — very much concerned about the decline of community in London's inner city areas. He campaigns actively for reversing the deterioration of the urban environment, and for solving London's housing needs. He puts it this way:

"In our society, we have great affluence and great deprivation side by side — and deprivation amid affluence is the worst kind of poverty. In my diocese, are all the symptoms of deprivation in the inner city, where the traditional ties of community have broken down. We have above-average numbers of children in care, of youngsters drawn into juvenile delinquency, of truancy and illegitimacy, and of the unemployed. The old sense of community in Stepney has been destroyed by high-rise flats, the building of great motorways that carve up old neighbourhoods and leave areas desolate, and the lack of balance in the population as young people leave and the elderly stay behind. This decline of community must be of vital concern to Christians, because we know that community is essential for people if they are to know meaning and purpose in their lives."

The Church itself must be the "community that embodies the Gospel, a community of love and hope."

Along with this "challenge of the secular city", Bishop Huddleston sees the tragic divisions of race and colour, and the problem of world hunger, as "the three key issues facing Christianity in the world today." Certainly he believes that we in Britain cannot turn aside from these world issues, for they affect us no less than mankind. More than once, he has criticised British society, and many in the Church too, for wanting to be introspective, self-centred and preoccupied with our own affairs to the exclusion of the rest of mankind.

"We have only one Earth, but we still act as if we don't believe it. The Western nations, those presumed steeped in the Christian tradition, are the worst offenders. We need a fundamental loyalty to the planet Earth as human beings, and doubly so as Christians, for this is God's Creation. In our interdependent world, the truth of God that we are called to be one human family, and should love one another as such, is now obvious. The obdurate resistance of men to this truth, and the refusal to accept that mankind is indeed One Family, are massive evidence of original sin at work in our world."

"The conflicts of race and colour, dividing man, are massive challenges to human survival world-wide. Race hatred threatens the future of our own society, and the future of mankind internationally. When a British politician uses the issue of immigration for his own ends, he is heard not only in Britain, but in Africa, too — he is heard to attack all black men everywhere, for our interdependent world is linked by instant communication media."

He still sees what happens in South Africa as central to the race question, world-wide. "Although racism is found in many parts of the world, only in South Africa is it built into the very institutions and laws of the country. Britain has a special responsibility here. We have long historic ties with South Africa. Massive British investment upholds its system. So there is a special responsibility upon the British Churches to take issue with all those in this country who sustain the South African regime by their political and economic support. To do this, we must recognise that the motives and forces behind racism are the Anti-Christ, denying that man is made in the divine image."

Huddleston's forthright mesage of the Gospel in action for our day is by no means always well-received. He has been shouted down at a public meeting by British racists. Yet, for the most part, he is very deeply respected outside the Church, as well as being an inspiration to many Christians here and in Africa. In Stepney itself, many East Enders who don't go to church, and for that matter don't like some of his views either, admit his truly Christian qualities and admire the fact that "he lives among us" among the noise and dirt, and not in some cloistered ecclesiastical precinct.

To the children of Stepney, who cluster eagerly around him wherever he goes in the diocese, he is simply "our bish" — and that speaks volumes of trust, affection and loyalty!

Bishop Trevor Huddleston: Key facts
Born 1913. Educated Lancing School, Oxford University, Wells theological College. 1937: Ordained priest in the Church of England. Worked in a Swindon parish. Joined Community of the Resurrection, and professed monastic vows in 1941. 1943: Went to South Africa to be Priest-in-charge of Sophiatown and Orlando Anglican Missions, in Johannesburg diocese. 1956: returned to England. 1958-1960: Prior of the London House of the Community of the Resurrection. 1960-1968: Bishop of Masasi, in Tanzania. 1968: Appointed suffragan Bishop of Stepney. 1969: Vice-President of Anti-Apartheid Movement. *Books include: Naught for Your Comfort, The True and Living God, God's World.*

Building Community and Peace

Lord George Macleod

Lord George Macleod
Building Community and Peace

In the summer of 1938, ten men set out from Glasgow for a small island on the west coast of Scotland. The group comprised five clergymen and five craftsmen: their aim was to restore a ruin. Many of their friends thought the venture quite eccentric, but their leader was a man of vision. He felt called by God to rebuild an ancient abbey, and found a new kind of Christian community there.

His name was George Macleod, the place Iona — and his vision came true.

Born in 1895 of Scottish aristocratic background, and educated at Winchester public school and Oxford and Edinburgh universities, Macleod entered the Church of Scotland ministry, devoting himself for four years to the Edinburgh West End parish of St. Cuthbert's. Then came the challenge to go to Glasgow, to become minister in the industrial slum parish of Govan. In the terrible Depression years of the 1930's, a time of mass unemployment, grinding poverty, wretched over-crowding and much personal hopelessness, what was the relevance of the Church?

"The Parish Church was still a patterned entity in a heavily over-crowded slum district. Even if adults did not go to church, it was still 'the thing' to send all their children. When I arrived in Govan, my parish had ten thousand in it — you could walk around it in fifteen minutes! — and the church membership allegedly three thousand. After an intensive visiting campaign, we cut the real membership down to seventeen hundred. I remember we had eighty adult baptisms! Over and above the membership, we had a thousand young people in our Sunday schools and bible classes."

For many, Macleod brought the worship of the church alive again. For many, too, it was his work among the unemployed that caught the imagination: he set up projects to provide them with work, organised clubs, and got them to give voluntary labour to build a camping place for young people at Fingalton Mill, in the countryside to the south of Glasgow. Amid the overcrowded Govan tenements, Macleod brought new hope with all kinds of community facilities. He tells of those days:

"At the centre of the overcrowded district stood the Pearce Institute. I was unmarried at the time and four of us (two assistants and a youth leader and myself) lived in the top flat. There was a gym, a men's club, a hall for six hundred, classrooms and other facilities. It was there we really got to know 'the unemployed' and developed a new relation, 'dog-collar to muffler.' That was the germ that made the Iona idea grow."

For he was realising it was not enough for the Church to 'do good works' among the needy. It had to give new meaning to their lives in the deepest way. In a world torn by industrial strife, could the Church pioneer new forms of human community, bringing men together? George Macleod perceived that a new unity of work and worship was needed — and a ruin on a remote island proved the key.

"I was 'nudged' by God to set about the rebuilding of Iona. On holiday every August, while a minister in Govan, the ruined Abbey seemed to beckon me every time I passed or entered it. St. Columba, who brought Christianity to Scotland in the sixth century, had established the first Abbey on Iona. The buildings had been in ruins for hundreds of years, but from 1905 to 1910 the Abbey Church had been restored for worship. My father had been Honorary Treasurer of the restoration fund, and I heard much about the project as a boy. Now in 1938, Iona seemed ideal for a corporate witness between clergy and craftsmen to build together, each learning from the other about the real meaning of weekday and the original meaning of Sunday."

"When we landed we built huts to live in during the following seasons, and during that summer of 1938 we plotted how we would start the rebuilding. Sir James Lithgow, the Govan shipbuilder, gave us our first £5000 to get going. The idea was that young ministers just out of training would join us for two years, build all summer with the craftsmen, and then go and work as assistants for the rest of the two years in *industrial* parishes (and not fashionable West End parishes!) In the next year, 1939, a new lot of ministers, and mostly the same craftsmen — who had gone back to their ordinary work in winter — began building the Abbey, starting with the Library."

"We all wore the same 'uniform' — a double-breasted blue suit, blue shirt and blue tie, a fisherman's Sunday garb, being the island symbol of industry. We all went unerringly to morning and evening service each day, and all unerringly in that uniform at the evening service; for years on end, with a different group of clergy each year and a recognisably similar group of builder artisans. We breakfasted at seven-thirty, had morning service at eight, then worked throughout the morning and afternoon. Three afternoons a week the clergy met together to discuss worship, ministry and pastoralia. Very soon, visitors started crowding in from all over Britain and beyond, and we started parallel youth camps from industrial parishes."

The pace of rebuilding quickened after the Second World War, and the Iona Community grew. The monastic building was restored, and became the centre of the Community's life. The members of the Community, who include both clergy and laymen, commit themselves to live and work at Iona for regular periods, while continuing their regular jobs for the rest of their time. The idea is that the spirit of Iona, its worship and common fellowship, will flow out through its members into all walks of life. Members also commit themselves to a common discipline of prayer and Bible study, the planned use of their time and money (including giving to poor Third World nations), work for peace, and attendance at Community meetings. The Iona Community is directly active on the Scottish mainland, and elsewhere too, in Industrial Mission, and a wide range of youth and community work activities, including summer camps for Borstal lads, and the Community House in Glasgow.

Geoge Macleod himself was Leader of the Iona Community from 1938 till 1967, and still keeps in very close touch, visiting the island at least six times each year. Over the years, many thousands of pilgrims and tourists have come to Iona, and they are still coming, as he told me: "In 1975, fifteen hundred people came, for retreat or conference, for at least a week, to live in the Abbey. Some twelve hundred teenagers came to our adjacent Youth Camp, and worshipped with us daily in the Abbey. And counting the many helpers who came, to be cooks, gardeners, guides and helpers in the canteen, we had over three thousand altogether in that year, and about the same number last year, 1976. What a potential if we can just focus the 'New Word' for our time — Jesus' Word!"

For the Founder of the Iona Community, that means peace.

In the First World War, as a young Captain in the Argyll and Sutherland Highlanders, George Macleod won the Military Cross and the Croix de Guerre — but subsequently renounced everything to do with militarism and violence, becoming a dedicated Christian pacifist. Appropriately, the common discipline of the Iona Community lays strong emphasis on Christian work for a peaceful world, in activities ranging from action for racial harmony in Britain to campaigns for nuclear disarmament. For many years, George Macleod has devoted much of his tireless energy to Christian peace-making. "I regard the Anti-Bomb campaign as the most important of my life," he told me. "I was very much a loner for years in ecclesiastical Scotland, but now everyone is urgently asking about the nuclear danger." A former President of the International Fellowship of Reconciliation, he was awarded a life peerage by Labour Prime Minister Harold Wilson in 1967, not least for his consistent dedication to the cause of peace. As Lord Macleod of Fuinary in Morven, he urges the dangers of nuclear war in the House of Lords. As a former moderator of the Church of Scotland, he sounds forth the message of peace at its General Assembly in Edinburgh. From pulpits and political platforms, on Iona pilgrimages and anti-H Bomb marches, in Britain, America and across the Commonwealth, he has preached the message of peace — and still does so, proclaiming his belief that only a revived Church can save mankind from the terrible harvest of war and violence.

"It is difficult to imagine how peace can be built. An unprecedented 'take off' in the perfection of novel deadly weapons has taken place. I don't think the full horror of the developing crisis has really entered the consciousness of most of us. Certainly the Churches show little sign of it. The 1975 Report of the Disarmament Study group of the International Peace Research Association of Oslo, prepared for the Churches' Commission on International Affairs, pointed out that 'nuclear arms, long thought of as deterrent only, have been stockpiled in absurd quantity.' Now eight nations possess nuclear weapons. In eight years forty nations will have nuclear power; it requires but six months to convert such to warlike purposes. The restraints which have contained nuclear weapon proliferation are progressively crumbling. Since the 'Non-Proliferation Treaty' was signed, nuclear arsenals have quadrupled!"

Lord Macleod reminds us of a fearful fact: "There is now the equivalent of ten tons of TNT available for each human being on earth; tens of thousands of nuclear bombs with a cumulative explosive power over a million times that of the Hiroshima atomic bomb."

The nuclear threat is not the only danger. The ever-increasing expenditure on both nuclear and so-called 'conventional' weapons by Britain and other major industrial nations, distorts the world's economic development, and hinders the conquest of poverty in the Third World. The real enemies are poverty, under-development, malnutrition, disease and ignorance — but the squandering of money and scientific research on military preparations does nothing to conquer these enemies!

"Western spending on arms was around £75 thousand million in 1975, Russian spending around £60 thousand million. Britain spent nearly £5000 million in that year, and sold £450 millions-worth to other nations — but total British Government aid to developing countries was only £300 million. The world is spending annually fifteen times as much on armaments as on all aid from the Western countries to the developing nations. In 1975 China spent over £600 million on nuclear power for warlike purposes. India, with its terrible problems of starvation, has entered the nuclear race 'to keep the balance' — and now Pakistan, frightened of India, seeks 'nuclear parity.' Thus the danger spreads, in the name of the balance of power."

George Macleod, prophet of peace, believes the Church has lost a lot of moral authority by failing to be uncompromising in its opposition to all war. Former Christian arguments for the 'Just War' have become outdated in the age of nuclear destruction.

"We all know, in our hearts, that in modern circumstances a Just War is an impossibility. Only the Church has within it the moral and spiritual resources to face the crisis of violence: the Church's potential is enormous, but its effects are nonetheless pallid. If violence is to be counted out, the commitment to non-violence is so demanding, that only deep faith in the Power of the Cross can result in ultimately effective action. We must return to the Early Church and its witness to pacifism. Pacifism is now central to the Christian faith, if that faith — in fact and not merely in hymns — is to become the salvation of our atomic world. The Church lives in its own small, ecclesiastical circles, while the world is going to hell. We have become too spiritual in a 'holy, holy' sense, whereas we should be Biblically holy — that means facing up to the totality of life, in the power of the Cross."

George Macleod's Christian vision for peace springs from an almost mystical understanding of how Christ unites Spirit and Matter, the world of spiritual things and the world of everyday affairs. "We say 'Jesus is Lord' — and, biblically, Lord means the Warden of the Loaf. The Final Judgement, of who is destined for Heaven and for Hell, a spiritual issue, is about the nations being gathered to be divided as sheep from goats, according to whether they have fed the hungry and clothed the naked. So all this is 'politics' — how we deal with each other in this world. Biblically, this New Obedience is symbolised by the Transfiguration story, when Jesus spoke with the Spiritual world (Moses and Elijah) at the same time as with the Material (Peter, James and John on the Mountain Top). Jesus became translucent, the 'At-one-ment' between Spirit and Matter, declaring the material as potentially spiritual, for in Christ, Spirit and Matter are one. We are shocked to remind ourselves that August 6th is the Feast of the Transfiguration — the date when, in 1945, the first Atomic Bomb was dropped on Nagasaki."

Yet George Macleod is not pessimistic: he believes the Church is on the threshold of a great revival, in the power of the Holy Spirit. As the Church rediscovers "the truth and power of Pentecost," it will be awakened to deeper personal commitment, political responsibility, and a pacifist witness, he believes.

"In its first three hundred years, the Church was small, faithful, joyous and persecuted by the state. It was pacifist, and lived in the power of Pentecost. After Constantine, the Church was promoted and patronised by the State, and became its servant. Now all that has ended. The modern state is the child of the secular, obedient to supra-national companies. The Church becomes relegated to 'fringe benefits' such as baptism and marriage. We are at the end of an age — yet, suddenly, the Spirit is breaking through again!"

"The Holy Spirit is not for our manipulation. We are to lay ourselves open, personally and corporately, and all the time, to his guidance. Unless we are personally committed, the wind of the Spirit cannot blow through us. The radical nature of the Church's current situation is almost parallel to the time of the Gospel itself. It is certainly true, as in Bible times, that only a revolution can restore both justice and mercy to our world. But to proceed simply at the political level would at once submerge each of us in secularity, so vast are the issues, unless we have ourselves been revolutionised and are prepared to be daily open to Bible study, prayer and costly fellowship."

Tall and erect, at eighty-two Lord Macleod is still a commanding figure, a powerful orator, and a humorous conversationalist. No remote ecclesiastic, he is easy to talk to. A lover of his native Scotland, he finds much inspiration from its ancient Celtic saints, particularly Iona's original founder, Columba.

"Columba said: 'Iona of my heart, Iona of my love, where there is praying of monks, there will be lowing of cattle: but Iona shall be as it was, ere the world come to an end'."

We can draw inspiration from the saints of the past, but the Church must always live for the future. Thus with his awesome vision of Peace and Pentecost, Lord George Macleod of Fuinary, truly one of the great Christian prophets of our century, challenges the Churches and Christians everywhere:

"When the Spirit came in power, Christians had all things in common, and the Gospel was preached to all nations gathered together. It was personal commitment to Christ, and it was political. We've forgotten that. When Christ was transfigured, He broke the false divisions of flesh and spirit, body and soul — so there should be no dichotomy of Church and world, religion and politics. We must each of us be humbled by this fresh wind of the Spirit that has come to lift us up from the nadir our civilisation has reached. It is for the traditional Churches now, ecumenically, to realise the Bible offer of Pentecost to be present, personal, political and pacifist, and so show forth men in every land the New Society of Non-Violent Revolution in the name of Christ. This alone will defeat the coming pollution, be it spiritual or physical."

George Macleod: Key facts
Born 1895. Educated Winchester School, Oxford and Edinburgh. Became a Church of Scotland minister in Edinburgh (1926-30) and Govan, Glasgow (1930-38). 1938: Founded the Iona Community (Leader of the Iona Community, 1938-67). 1957-58: Moderator of the General Assembly of the Church of Scotland. 1963: President of the International Fellowship of Reconciliation. 1967: Created Life Peer — Lord Macleod of Fuinary in Morven. 1968-71: Rector of Glasgow University. *Books include: Govan Calling, Speaking the Truth in Love, We shall Rebuild, Only One Way Left.*

A New Way of Praying

Michel Quoist

Michel Quoist
A New Way of Praying

A dozen years ago, a small book of prayers by a French priest appeared in English translation, and went on sale in Britain. Hardly an event to catch the headlines — indeed, the priest himself had been very reluctant about publishing the prayers at all, thinking they would be of little interest outside his own parish at Le Havre. Yet almost overnight the book became a best -seller. It was acclaimed as an exciting new way of doing prayer, as a spiritual masterpiece, as the great popular religious classic for the second half of the 20th century.

Soon, it was widely read outside the Catholic Church. Anglicans quoted from it. The prayers were read from many Free Church pulpits. Churchmen of all denominations were soon using its memorable phrases across the world. It went into more than twenty-five languages, including Japanese and Slovakian. To date, over five million copies have been sold.

The book, of course, is *Prayers of Life*. Its author Abbé Michel Quoist, the French Roman Catholic priest who has done more than anyone else to make prayer real for everyday for modern people. He has given us a whole new way of understanding prayer, as we reflect before God on the world around us. Quoist's prayers have such a strong and immediate appeal because their God is no far-away cosmic force, but a power and presence in the ordinary affairs of life. In a quite remarkable way, in his books and preaching, Michel Quoist takes God out of the mists of the supernatural — and discovers Him anew amid the shelves and checkouts of the supermarket. He takes the Cross of Christ out of a hallowed stained-glass window — and sets it up fairly and squarely amid the high-street shops and office-blocks of the modern city, amid race riots and broken marriages, among the playgrounds and work-shops of our world — and on its scarred battlefields. For Michel Quoist, the Holy Spirit is for real in our everyday world, so prayer is for real, too. His prayers find the Holy Spirit not in pious clichés nor escapist mysticism, but blowing in all sorts of unlikely places, like football matches, slums and Tube trains.

When I met Michel Quoist for the first time, he told me how the *Prayers of Life* first came to be written. I wasn't altogether surprised to learn they were not born in the secluded atmosphere of a cloister or the academic calm of a study. "I did not sit at my desk and compose them 'out of the air'," the Abbé Quoist explained. "They were not written in any academic or narrowly pious fashion, but in response to the needs of people in special situations, and in talking with those people. I wrote the final version of each of the *Prayers*, but each theme had already been discussed at length with a local parish group, such as workers or students, mostly at my native town, the port of Le Havre."

For many years he was senior Roman Catholic youth chaplain for the Le Havre region, as well as holding key posts in Action Catholique. He became a familiar figure on the quayside and in colleges, and as well-known to young shipyard and dockside workers as to students — but he never confined his ministry to youth. Out of the hurly-burly experience of sharing many people's seeking and finding of God amid the ordinary problems and joys of life, came *Prayers of Life*. So it's no surprise you find prayers focusing on telephones and tractors, housing and hospitals, delinquency and young love, and the Stations of the Cross for 20th century Man.

If once we thought prayers about everyday life unusual, we no longer do so. Michel Quoist has educated us all! From factories to five pound notes, bricklayers to blackboards, and fences to funerals — Quoist finds the images of the divine among the daily events of life. He weaves a tapestry of prayer about the practical. He has a genius for combining reverent praise and petition to God with an unsentimental facing up to life as it really happens: the emptiness of a house after the wife has walked out, or the expectations of young people in love.

Quite typically of the man, Michel Quoist remains very modest about the worldwide appeal of his books, and how it all happened. "I began to write a few prayers for parish use. Then, to my surprise, I found them turning up in duplicated parish sheets in Marseilles, Rouen and elsewhere, so I decided I might as well publish them."

"Of course, I wrote in French, for French Catholics." The rapid worldwide appeal of Quoist's prayers across the frontiers of church tradition and nationality alike, shows that Christians today are seeking a new way of praying. Michel Quoist has helped millions to find that new way.

"I find, to my astonishment, that many people who are neither French nor Catholic like to read my books! Naturally, it makes me happy, and I suppose the reason is that, quite without intending it, in trying to answer questions about man's spiritual search, the books speak to many people outside my country and outside Catholicism, because that search is universal today."

Prayers of Life was not his first book. Nor was he a stranger to the secular world before he began composing prayers uplifting the everyday world to God. Michel Quoist's experience includes deep research into the condition of modern man in the great cities of today. After being ordained priest in 1947, he won high academic laurels for his research into urban sociology, notably with studies of working-class city life. His books *The City and Man* and *The Urban Inquest* made a distinctive contribution to thinking about urban planning and development in post-war France, even at official Ministry of Reconstruction levels. He received his doctorate in Social and Political Sciences from the Catholic Institute in Paris. In 1954 the French Geographical Society awarded him the Prix Jansen for his study of a Paris working-class district. Six years later, the Abbé Quoist was honoured with the Grand Prix of the Rouen Academy of Sciences. His theology and life of prayer are very closely interwoven with his very deep understanding of contemporary urban man and city society, resulting both from his research and many years of living and ministering pastorally among working people. His sympathies are very much with their social and political hopes and aims. He put it this way when we discussed a Christian understanding of politics: "I believe that socialist political and economic structures are more moral, and tend to be more truly Christian, than capitalist ones. Yet it is certainly true that a political revolution remains incomplete, and can become hollow, without a spiritual transformation. Once, I visited Cuba. There, I met the government minister for Religious Affairs. I told him that as a Christian I strongly approved many of the social and economic changes I had seen in Cuba, but that I had found no 'new men.' Without such men, spiritually transformed, any revolution would ultimately fail."

Having spent so much of his life serving God among young people — Quoist was senior youth chaplain at Le Havre for seventeen years — talking with them and listening to them, Quoist believes that they have a very special responsibility in the task of changing the world, to make it more Christ-like. They should not be put off by difficulties. Their quest must be powered by the Holy Spirit. They must not fly off into pious escapism.

"In the 1960's many young people began to become aware of their responsibilities for the world, and among them some Christians realised their Faith was not just a matter of commandments but essentially one of love — not only personal love, but love in the social and political structures, too. So the young began to struggle for a better world. In

1968 youth movements in fifty countries rose to declare that the world
was full of evil, that man and society must be changed. They had
discovered that our consumer society doesn't satisfy the deepest needs
of the heart. Some wanted to destroy, others to plan to build anew. But
that situation has gone. Those young people found building a new
world much more difficult than they had imagined. Oppressive social
and political forces hurt and crushed them."

Michel Quoist believes that many young people, and people of all
ages inside and outside the Church, remain deeply dissatisfied with the
materialism of our consumer society. Today, the danger is that they
may try to escape from it, into the escapism of pleasure or even the self-
destruction of drugs. Or, if Christians, they might flee into a world of
pseudo-piety and shallow mysticism.

"Increasingly, for many young people the question is no longer 'how
to live?' but 'why live?' They are searching for that beyond, that extra
dimension. Their search is taking them into all sorts of unlikely places.
A preoccupation with finding God directly, has the danger of an
evasion of the world. You can be so preoccupied with seeing heaven,
that you do not see the world about you! Yet the search for God should
never mean an evasion of the world. That is as incomplete as activism
without God. For God is not distant: He came to us in Love made Man.
As part of our quest for — and with — God, we must be involved in
changing the world."

Abbé Quoist stresses that the Church must be positive in its
proclamation of the Gospel among young people.

"It is very important for the Church to declare that the whole of life
belongs to God, and that nothing is outside His care and concern.
Young people want to live life to the full. They want to say 'Yes!' to
life. The Church must make clear that with Christ they can say 'Yes!'
to life, in fulfilment of life with Him. The implications of this are much
wider than we usually think: *Christ wants a new man in a new world.*
So, as young people see Christ at the heart of the world, they are
challenged to say — 'Yes! I'll join you!' "

If we are to become new men and women for the new world built in
the spirit and power of Christ, we must know "the Total Christ."

"We can know Christ in his two dimensions: first, the historic Jesus
of Nazareth, whom we know as we read the Gospels — we should read
them like a love letter from Christ to us — and with whom we can have
a profound personal friendship. Secondly, we must know the Christ —
crucified, risen and alive among men. So this is no mere Christianity of
the head alone, but the total Christ in all his Body. If we only know
Christ by his mind, and not in his whole mystical body, we mutilate

him. But if we only know him as feet and hands, and don't learn of the mind of Christ, then we decapitate him. We must meet and know Christ in his head and all his limbs, in personal love and in sacrificial service."

The Christian has to face the fact that many people who rarely, if ever, go to church, indeed many who would definitely not call themselves Christians, can and do live lives of sacrificial service to their fellow men. They may be doctors, nurses, teachers, social workers, or members of other caring professions. They may be in trades unions or business or in some charity or welfare organisation. Their motivation may be a non-religious philosophy, such as Humanism or Marxism. Often, they claim no particular religion or philosophy at all. How can we understand this, if as Christians we believe that God is at work in the secular, everyday world, in all sorts of ways? I put the question to Michel Quoist. His reply was characteristically comprehensive.

"If a person, such as a humanist, is giving himself for his fellows, if he is advancing the values of the Gospel, love, joy, peace and justice among men, then that person is certainly within the work of the Kingdom. But his understanding is deficient in that he does not acknowledge Christ, who is Risen and at work in the world. It is not only the humanist who can be deficient like this: many Christians do not grow in maturity of faith. An old lady may centre her faith on the crucifix. Another person may never get beyond Christianity as moral obligation. Another may know Christ in a personal relationship, but not acknowledge him as risen and alive in the world, creative among men. Christians are all at different stages of maturity in their understanding and relationship to Christ. So the humanist is at an immature stage, too. The humanist needs to acknowledge Christ in his fulness, and so does the Christian. We all need to realise that eternal life begins here, in this world."

Michel Quoist's understanding and practice of prayer is very much part of the great movement of change and renewal that has swept through the Roman Catholic Church over the past two decades. The life and work of Pope John XXIII, and the achievements of the Second Vatican Council, gave the movement its greatest impetus. A key aspect of all this change within Roman Catholicism has been a very real "rediscovery of the Bible". Quoist stresses that a proper use of the Bible, alongside a fresh way of praying, is essential for learning a spirituality for today's secular world.

"By reading the Bible, especially the Gospels, we meet therein the Jesus of Nazareth, and get to know him, his mentality, his outlook on life, his understanding of man, and indeed all about him. In this way, we develop a profound personal knowledge and relationship with him. But the Bible must be related to life! The Risen Christ is alive in the world — so we must not only pause to reflect upon passages from the Bible, but upon 'slices of life,' too, relating them together, and to the will of the Risen Christ for us." He believes that as Christians we can check our lives against Christ's calling, by asking ourselves key questions:

"What is Jesus saying, demanding, waiting for me to do, in response to this situation in life?"

"How can he through me, in this small part of life where I am, build the Kingdom of his Father?"

"Was I — am I — faithful, to what he wants?"

"Bible and life must go together. As we know the Jesus of Nazareth as the Risen Christ, we discover him in life, and as we see him in life, we discover him more deeply in the Bible."

Another achievement of the Second Vatican Council was a new emphasis on the importance of the lay people in the Church. Here the work of the Abbé Quoist is again very relevant: although his prayers are much used by clergy, his main concern is for lay people in the Church to develop an authentic spirituality for today. He puts it this way:

"The laity participate in Christ's work by their engagement in the world. The Christian must look at life and, when he sees Christ, must go out to meet him and work with him wherever he is — among the poor of the world, wherever the values of the Gospel are being advanced among men, and not only in Church activities. Many Christians are really outside life, withdrawn into their churches. It is a very real temptation to laity who are much involved in church work to think that the Church is more important than the world. Just as Jesus was first of all a man among men, so the layman must first live in the secular world and then reflect upon that life in the world, rather than withdrawing from the world to reflect. The traditional saints of the Church, such as Catherine of Sienna, Theresa of Avila, John of the Cross, were really saints 'out of this world' — their saintliness was a direct 'vertical' meeting with God. But the vocation of the laity is quite different: it is to a saintliness that lies in their *belonging to life*."

In our personal relationship with the Risen Christ, through reflection on the Bible and life, and by being involved in the everyday affairs of the world with and for God, we know the "total Christ" more and more fully, and avoid the danger of "other-worldly spirituality."

"Everything depends on your vision of faith in Christ. If you think of Christ solely as the one who came from God to the world and then returned to God, then your spirituality will be 'heavenly' and forgetful of this world. However, if you understand that Christ is Risen, then you believe he is alive and among us now. He said 'I am with you always,' and the mystery of the Living Christ is unfolding in human history. If you grasp that vision of faith in Christ, you will try to meet him in his work for the whole of life, in order to work with him. Once and for all he saved the world perfectly, and as the mystery of his salvation unfolds in the world, he is always at work saving man — but in a real sense he can't save us without ourselves. Christ invites us to join with him in the mystery of salvation."

A true spirituality for the secular world means discovering the work of Christ amid the needs of the world.

"We must take seriously what Christ said about his presence among us, so we know how and when to meet him. He said he would be present when groups gather in his name, and when we meet for the Eucharist. He further identified himself with the poor of the world, so we meet him among the hungry, the down-and-outs, and those in prison. Today, Christ's 'I was hungry' does not refer only to those without food — though it certainly means the peoples of the Third World — but in our society must also mean 'I had a low wage,' 'I was black,' 'I had a small old age pension.' "

It is the whole world that our vision of Christ's concern must encompass — and that includes the poor nations of Africa, Asia and Latin America. Michel Quoist knows their conditions at first hand. As General Secretary of the French Episcopal Committee for Latin America for several years, he toured that continent more than a dozen times: "Its enormous potential is exhilarating, its problems are vast, and the conditions of many of its people appalling."

He believes the Church must be committed to justice and development for the Third World, and see that as part of the ongoing creative work of Christ.

"As Christians, we need a fuller understanding of Christ's ongoing work in Creation. When men and nations remain under-developed through lack of opportunities for educational and economic advance, it is frustration of God's purpose to bring His Creation to fulfilment. It is sin — and we must take account of the collective sin of the world, as well as personal sin. The road to Jericho today, the road of the Good Samaritan, goes through every under-developed country. It is no use the Church simply sending bags of rice: we must understand the problem in its full dimensions. Amid hunger, racism and war, Christ is continuing to suffer and struggle with evil. As we commit ourselves entirely to share his pain, his suffering and his love, he involves us in his plan for the redemption of the world."

Abbé Quoist's ability to write books of Christian prayer and reflection read by millions in over thirty countries derives from his own deep insights into the life of Jesus Christ for today, and his wide experience of all kinds of people. For, after his many years of pastoral and mission work among young workers and students, Quoist spent the years from 1970 to 1976 as priest-in-charge of the Sainte-Marie parish in Le Havre. "I tried to think not only of the Christian community there, but of the whole human community, including the many who lived right outside the Church," he told me. Especially, he developed a caring ministry among the elderly. Now, he is at the Centre of Catholic Action in Le Havre, and is in charge of the diocesan Vocations Service, with pastoral and educational care for all those young people wanting to become priests or nuns. Because of his books and the world wide interest they continue to arouse, Abbé Michel Quoist travels much, preaching, speaking at conferences and conducting retreats.

Dynamic, but slight of stature, with an easy smile, a ready sense of humour and a twinkle in his eye, Michel Quoist is as memorable to meet as he is inspiring to read. His appeal spans all age groups and all denominations. Of course, he didn't stop with *Prayers of Life: The Christian Response, Christ is Alive!* and *Meet Christ and Live!* are important books of Christian insight and devotion, beloved of many hundreds of thousands of readers in many countries. Read them all, and reflect upon his prayers — for in so doing, your own prayer life will surely be enriched, and your whole horizon of God's activity and purpose in the world widened. For the Abbé Michel Quoist points us to a new way of seeing the world:

"If only we knew how to look at life as God sees it, We should realise that nothing is secular in the world, but that everything contributes to the building of the kingdom of God. To have faith is not only to raise one's eyes to God to contemplate him; it is also to look at the world — but with Christ's eyes."

(Prayers of Life, p.10)

Abbé Michel Quoist: Key facts
Born Le Havre 1921. Father died young, so he had to work at 14: very active in 'Action Catholique'. Ordained priest 1947. Won Doctorate in Social and Political Sciences, Institute Catholique 1954, Prix Jansen of the French Geographical Society 1960, the Grand Prix at Rouen Academy of Sciences. 1953-1970: youth Chaplain in Le Havre with 'Action Catholique'; Gen. Sec. of the French Episcopal Committee for Latin America. 1970-76: Parish Priest, Sainte Marie, Le Havre. Since 1976: Director of Vocations Service, Le Havre diocese. Books include: *Prayers of Life, The Christian Response, Christ is Alive! Meet Christ and Live!*

Church in the City

Bishop David Sheppard

Bishop David Sheppard
Church in the City

David Sheppard, the Anglican bishop of Liverpool, first hit the headlines as an outstanding cricketer. At the age of eighteen, he was playing first class county cricket for Sussex. Over the next six years he was to captain both Sussex and the Cambridge University team, and soon attracted the attention of the England selectors. He played for England twenty-two times, and was captain of the Test team in 1954. It was a dazzling success story as a top-line cricketer. His sheer craftsmanship as a batsman delighted countless thousands of spectators and dismayed dozens of bowlers for fifteen seasons. It was a career at the wicket with memorable dramatic moments, too. On a July day in 1956 at Old Trafford, called back from his Islington curacy to play for England, he hit a century against Australia and saved the Ashes.

Yet Sheppard, Test hero and schoolboy's summer idol, was very different from other famous cricketers. An evangelical Christian, he decided to devote himself to the service of God and his fellow men within the parish ministry of the Church of England: even while playing for county and country, he had become ordained. For him, there was no separation between his religion and his sport — the game was part of his discipleship, though not in any 'holy, holy' way!

"My Christian faith became something first hand after I started at University, at 20 years of age. I was already deeply involved in cricket, having been given my county cap for Sussex that year. So in a real sense cricket was the milieu in which I had to work out my faith. I believed God wanted Christian cricketers as well as Christians elsewhere. I'm grateful that I had to work out what it meant to follow Christ in what was certainly not a churchgoing circle. I like to think I was a keen cricketer because I became a Christian — not in the sense that I would make a big score if I was fully prayed up — but as a loyal and honest member of the team. And there is an element of ordeal in big cricket, and perhaps my faith helped me to cope with that," David Sheppard told me.

Cambridge and Test Cricket would have been a ready passport to 'fashionable' parishes, but two years as assistant curate at St. Mary's,

Islington, awakened him to the problems of the Church in working-class areas. From then onwards, he determined to devote himself to the tough task of urban mission.

David Sheppard's first key experience of tackling inner city problems as part of Christian mission came when he was Warden of the Mayflower Family Centre in Canning Town, a working-class district in East London. This Christian residential and community centre is "dedicated to loving service to the neighbourhood," particularly reaching out to local young people through its club activities. Getting East End youngsters away for weekends in countryside fresh air, and sport and recreation at the Centre, were not for David Sheppard primarily a means of attracting teenagers into the pews, but a practical way of saying "God as Creator is concerned about the quality of people's lives." But the emphasis had to be on 'not being stuffy!'

"The Church must never grow too respectable. Two lads who wanted to go to church here waited outside to see if people were allowed in without ties. After several had come in without ties, then they joined the congregation."

He did not run the Mayflower Centre as a Christian social work centre. "In one sense, that would have been easy. But it was not our job to be amateur social workers — there were plenty of proper facilities to which we could refer those in need. Rather, our target was the 'happy pagan': by preaching the Gospel to the average man and woman, the whole community could become more loving and caring." It was easier said than done. In Canning Town, like many other inner city working-class areas, the Church has been in retreat for decades, and traditional methods of services and meetings have long since ceased to attract the vast majority. David Sheppard recalls: "Amid many frustrations, God was teaching us that the Church needs far fewer meetings but much more meeting with people. A men's group failed, so we tried home meetings. They didn't work out in the organised way we expected, but people began using their homes."

For two years, David Sheppard and his wife Grace kept every Thursday evening free for being with non-church couples. "The Centre just seemed to throw up the contacts. We went visiting, the couples began slowly to come to our homes in return. We rarely talked narrowly about religious things, but I made a point of always leading a half-hour discussion of some moral issue at some late stage in the evening. This kind of visiting is a change of pattern for the neighbourhood, for people in Canning Town are not used to home visiting in this sense, but rather to spontaneous talk on doorsteps. That is fine, but when you are twenty-five stories up in high-rise blocks there are no doorsteps in the sky. We had to develop new patterns — and I believe the Gospel causes new patterns of life to happen. After eighteen months, couples began coming to 'Searching Groups' for more specific Christian discussion, and then the groups went on happening in a rather random way as couples visited each other in their homes."

Through that and similar experiences, David Sheppard learned a lot about the new style of mission the Church would have to develop, if it were to have any chance of success in inner city areas. "At Mayflower, we had to learn how to create talking groups, so that people could have confidence in themselves, long before they will talk about the things of God. Discussion had to be free-ranging. I didn't correct people, though I tried to guide discussion. As people were fully accepted for themselves, and not judged by their formal education or lack of it, they began to respond and grow in self-confidence. A woman once said of one of our groups 'You don't feel stupid here!' But all that didn't deny the aspect of Christian teaching: the Good News has to be proclaimed, but not necessarily in the traditional, formalised ways."

At Mayflower, too, David Seppard learned a truth that has become widely accepted for Christian mission — that the Church must take seriously the cultural background of people, whether working-class or middle-class. Sheppard puts it this way: "The Church is usually tidy, institutional, regular, and to do with books. Canning Town, and places like it, are spontaneous, disorganised, non-bookish — and we tried to reflect that at Mayflower. If Christianity is identified with books it becomes identified with 'Them' rather than 'Us', for the working-class person. As long as the Church is associated exclusively with middle-class culture, it will mean little to those of the very different — and I stress different, not better or worse — working-class culture. The Church must recognise the high intelligence and leadership potential in working-class urban areas like Canning Town. Our Mayflower experience proved that time and again."

In 1969, David Sheppard crossed the Thames southwards to become Bishop of Woolwich, as suffragan to the Bishop of Southwark, with responsibility for the eastern half of that diocese stretching from riverside Greenwich to affluent Surrey commuterland. The Sheppard family deliberately chose to live in working-class Peckham, in a rambling Victorian house in a side street off the Old Kent Road, "so as not to be remote from ordinary people."

"Of course, this is where I should be living, because my speciality is urban mission, and more specifically the Church's task in the working-class areas of the big cities. So I see London particularly from the inner city point of view," he told me. For the Church of England, as for all the Christian denominations, the inner city has changed very much in recent decades, resulting in a different context for Christian mission, with new problems and new priorities. Parallel with sweeping urban redevelopment and the building of new estates and high-rise flats, traditional churchgoing dwindled and old Christian loyalties diminished. Declining recruitment for the Christian ministry and falling finance for the upkeep of church buildings sharpened the crisis of the inner city Church. New attitudes, approaches and styles of the Church's ministry and presence are called for — and David Sheppard has been a leading advocate of such changes.

As Bishop of Woolwich, he readily saw the need to change the structures of parish life.

"I believe it is important to work at pastoral reorganisation, because the 'structure' of church life influences the kind of Christians we are. If a congregation of twenty adults has to maintain a complete set of church buildings, it feels it must run all the organisations that churches run. Every able-bodied adult will feel the pressure of loyalty to give a great deal of time just to keep the church going. It is not surprising if he becomes the kind of Christian who has no time for his family, his neighbours or community life — and so, too, that church becomes more and more out of touch with the community."

David Sheppard strongly believes that part of the answer is a 'team' approach to Christian ministry and priesthood.

"Other professions work in teams — why should not the Church have teams too? What does it say about the inadequacy of our faith that we find it so difficult sometimes to work together? Except in areas where church life is strong, I believe that it can destroy good clergy by putting them to serve alone in a parish. Clergy can draw much strength from a common prayer life and discipline, and regular unhurried staff meetings — though I'm not advocating that clergy live together. In a team ministry, it is good for different staff members to live in different parts of the parish."

"Under the traditional parish system, each church has a full plant, with church building, hall and vicarage. Particularly in the inner city, all this is harder and harder to maintain. If you unite parishes, and look at a larger area as a whole, it does not follow there is only one centre for church activities. You may well have one large parish church, but it won't have a monopoly of what the church does in that area."

Bishop Sheppard stresses there must be many expressions of church life in any locality — house groups, a shop front, and experiments like the Kidbrooke "coffee shop church." Developments in team ministry are easier to start in new or replanned areas, such as Thamesmead New Town, "but in older areas it is much more difficult to reorganise the parishes. It is always hurtful to a congregation to have to agree to see their building declared redundant, for they have invested so much of their Christian life there over so many years. Memories and sentimenal attachment have to be measured against the need to use the Church's resources in the most effective way, for the whole community, as well as for the Church. The purpose of reorganisation is not to replace neighbourhood-level Christian action with bigger units, but to make neighbourhood work more effective. Church building should always serve Christ's mission, and that certainly means the long-term loving of people in the local neighbourhood by the local Christians."

Worship, too, must be very varied, responding to the local needs. Within the broad framework of set 'Prayer Book' type services, there must be freedom to experiment, with local church people writing their own prayers, composing new hymns, and young people doing their own music, drama and dance — so that the local community can offer its aspirations to God in its own style.

In June 1975, David Sheppard became Bishop of Liverpool, a city dogged by massive problems of inner city decline, slum clearance, urban deprivation, unemployment, economic rundown and juvenile vandalism — yet a city also nationally renowned for the friendly spirit of its people, their distictive 'Scouse' humour, and their fanatical following for football!

A major reason for his appointment to the Liverpool diocese, one of the most important in the Church of England, was David Sheppard's widely-acknowledged and respected experience and understanding of the Church's task today in the inner areas of our great cities. To this problem, he has given a great deal of thought, and in 1974 wrote a very influential book on the subject, called *Built as a City*, significantly sub-titled "God and the Urban World Today." Among Christian leaders and local clergy and lay churchpeople alike, it has helped re-shape attitudes on urban mission and stimulated new approaches to the Church's activities and parish structures in the cities. Sheppard believes that a properly Biblical understanding of the Church's task must drive Christians out into society to help tackle its urgent problems — and, for him, they are particularly those of the city.

"As an evangelical, regarding Scripture as my first authority, I believe I have become more biblical, not less, through becoming concerned about housing, race and education. God as Creator is concerned about the whole quality of men's lives, not only with the personal conversion, important though that is. Of course, as a bishop, I must serve all traditions of churchmanship!"

David Sheppard is "radical, not revolutionary" in his approach, seeking to reform the Church to make it more effective for mission, and thus more effective in its obedience to God today. I asked him to define mission.

"Mission is a very wide word, including everything God sends us to do. He sends us out of an inward-looking church fellowship taken up simply with religious concerns, into mission in the world. Such mission includes concern about housing, education, community relations and racial discrimination, out of obedience to the sovereignty of God in Creation, for this is God's world. It also includes speaking about Christ and his claims at the timely moment. In the 'unchurched' areas of the inner city, there are no easy answers to the problems of mission. Special 'mission' events in the parish have their place: they sharpen the responsibility of the congregation to their local situation. But in the long run, the important thing is the long, slow slog of a church vis-a-vis its local community. Mission will not happen unless the church goes beyond its own life in active care into the neighbourhood."

In his role as a bishop, David Sheppard sees his job as "enabling and encouraging" inner city mission to take place, by helping the local Christian leaders, clergy and laity, to perceive their task more clearly, and by steadily pushing towards new parish structures with men and resources deployed to carry out that task.

"I long to see strong, locally-rooted churches in the inner city and in the great corporation estates, which are slices of inner city put elsewhere. By 'locally-rooted,' I mean that local people should become the leaders and decision-makers. This may mean a different style of church life from tidy, bookish suburban churches."

"I believe working-class people, and, for example, black people, will take the Church seriously if they see us standing up for justice even though that may be to our own disadvantage."

Easy to meet, with an open friendly manner and no time for standing on episcopal protocol, David Sheppard is a very attractive person — and certainly still very young-looking for his forty-eight years! Yet his apparently easy style does not mean he glosses over difficulties — the very reverse. His Gospel-based proclamation of justice for the inner city is forthright and uncompromising.

"People talk about a thousand cities of a million or more by the year 2000. For the Christian Churches urban mission should not be a marginal subject, but a burning, central issue. We talk about priority areas — that means those areas come first. If we are determined about where priority lies, we shall resist complaints about the unfairness of giving extra resources to such areas. Christians are committed to a distictive view of justice in human relations. It is not a demand for fairness for all, supposing all to begin from the same starting-line. The Old Testament idea of justice has a built-in bias in favour of those with greatest needs, the widow, the orphan, the foreigner, the oppressed. Christians have a distinctive part to play in conversations when grumbles are expressed about overseas aid, about world trading conditions which are less advantageous to us, or about positive discrimination in favour of the most deprived urban areas."

So David Sheppard, once the hero of the cricket field, is now an Anglican bishop in the vanguard of the Church's struggle for mission and social action in the inner cities of our land. He sees no contradiction between the two: the Gospel is for the whole of life.

"In many ways, the deepest rift in the Church nowadays is not between denominations or between high church and low church. It is between those on the one hand who feel we are called to change the structure of society and to care about the life of the whole community, and those on the other hand who feel we are called to bring individuals to faith in Christ and to build up the worshipping community. I believe this is a false posing of opposites. We are called to do both!"

David Sheppard: Key facts
Born 1929. Educated: Sherborne school; Trinity Hall, Cambridge; Ridley Hall Theological College. 1955-57: Assistant Curate, St. Mary's Anglican Church, Islington, (London). 1957-69: Warden of Mayflower Family Centre, Canning Town, east London. 1969-75: suffragan Bishop of Woolwich. 1975: Appointed Bishop of Liverpool. Cricket: played for Cambridge University (1950-52), Sussex (1947-62, captain 1953) and England (22 times) (1950-63). Captain of England in 1954. *Books*: *Parson's Pitch* and *Built as a City*.

Living for Unity

Brother Roger Schutz, Prior of Taizé

Brother Roger Schutz, Prior of Taizé
Living for Unity

Thirty-seven years ago, a young French Protestant went into a remote part of the Burgundy countryside, near the ancient ruined Abbey of Cluny, to pray and seek the will of God. To an outsider, it would have seemed a quite irrelevant and escapist thing to do. For the year was 1940. The panzer divisions of Nazi Germany had smashed France to sudden and total defeat. Across the channel, the fate of Britain, of the future of Western civilisation with it, hung dangerously in the balance. A terrible evil seemed to be engulfing Europe — hardly the time to go into religious retreat!

Yet that young Protestant, Roger Schutz, was not running away. He felt an overwhelming call "to wait upon God" and know his will. He glimpsed amid the darkness of his nation's fate, a new work for God for the future. Amid so much despair, he had to obey God's call to light a small candle of resurrection hope. So he bought a small house in a tiny Burgundy village, and began to pray. Soon he began action, too, courageously helping Jewish refugees to escape Nazi persecution by crossing into neutral Switzerland. He gathered around him the nucleus of a community of lay brothers. Together, they prayed and sought God's will. Forced for a time to leave by Gestapo pressure, by 1944 Roger Schutz had returned. He and a small group of lay brothers had become fired by a vision — a new Christian community dedicated to a new Church for a new humanity. Their community was to be a new monastic order, the first of its kind in the Protestant Churches since the Reformation, four hundred years earlier. The community was to be devoted to the ideal of Christian Unity — a bridge between long-separated Christian traditions, particularly a bridge between Roman Catholics and Protestants.

The name of that tiny, obscure French village where Roger Schutz felt called of God to establish the new community, was Taizé.

Today, over three decades later, Taizé is an inspiration to the whole Christian world. The Prior of Taizé, brother Roger Schutz, is one of the most loved, most influential, and most significant Christian leaders of our time. For he is a quite remarkable man leading a quite remarkable community. Every year, particularly in the summer months, tens of thousands of the young and not-so-young, from countries across Europe and the world, flock to Taizé. They come from every Christian tradition — Catholic, Protestant, Anglican, Orthodox, Pentecostal — and from none. For the most part, they live under canvas, camping out in the fields and on the Burgundy hillside around the massive concrete Church of the Reconciliation. They are welcomed by the Taizé brothers, who themselves have come from many Churches in many countries. Originally a Protestant Order, the Taizé community now includes some Roman Catholics, too. Often the brothers, like the visitors and regular worshippers, are drawn by the sheer magnetism of Roger Schutz himself. Certainly, his utter dedication to God and his utter simplicity of life, are immensely attractive.

The brothers bring their many and varied talents. Farmers, musicians, doctors, theologians, a famous potter and a computer expert, are found in their ranks. The Taizé Community is self support-ing. It markets Christian art and pottery, the famous Taizé records and devotional books — and farm produce. The brothers' use of the latest agricultural methods has helped farmers in the surrounding countryside to be more efficient. This very practical ministry is also part of Roger Schutz's vision of a Christian community devoted to the needs of the whole man. This means the brothers work both at Taizé itself, and in many parts of the world. At Taizé, they pray, worship and work together — and they minister to the vast crowds of guests and visitors, welcoming them, and being among them in order to give spiritual guidance and counsel as needed.

In the wider world, Taizé brothers are quietly at work in the slums and tension-torn ghettoes of big cities, and in many places of need. Often they are a sign of Christian unity: at Coventry Cathedral, for some years a group of Taizé brothers ran the Chapel of Unity — and worked in local factories! Other brothers have manned an ambulance-station in West Africa. Over all this very varied activity, Prior Schutz acts as wise director and inspiration.

To meet Roger Schutz is an unforgettable experience. His bright eyes reach to the very core of one's being, yet do so lovingly and car-ingly. One is conscious of being in the presence of a spiritual giant — that rare kind of person who combines great spiritual power with an immense gentleness, humility and simplicity of life. A deep quiet pervades his life-style. He has immense personal magnetism, possessing a quality of obviously attractive holiness which really does shine from his face. There is nothing of the remote 'guru' about him. Readily sensitive to the needs of all around him, he radiates an infectious joy of the Spirit.

I first met Prior Schutz at an Easter Sunday morning celebration of the Eucharist. Over two thousand of us had gathered before dawn, in the great Church of the Reconciliation, and as the sun began to rise over the Burgundy countryside, the doors of the church opened and a brother entered, bearing a great Easter candle from which we all lit our small candles. A great shout went up in the church: "Christ is Risen! He is Risen indeed!" After the worship, as we ate a simple breakfast of coffee and rolls, Prior Schutz moved among the crowds, talking to people, praying briefly with them, and being open to everyone's needs in a very remarkable way. His preaching of life in the Risen Christ was made doubly powerful by his own life-style of openness and holiness. When I met him again, on one of his rare visits to London, for a great meeting in St. Paul's Cathedral, I was struck by the sheer depth of his contacts with other people. He has an almost uncanny knack of sensing the needs and unspoken burdens of those around him. He is able to speak to a person's deepest needs, even upon the briefest acquaintance. Such qualities come only from a very close and prayerful relationship to God.

Schutz is no mystic escapist from the world, but he strongly attacks our modern Western civilisation for its materialism, joylessness and preoccupation with success. All these he sees as quite contrary to that abundant life as taught by Christ.

"Man today attempts to escape his guilt through the electrifying effects of consumer society, through seeking different ways of being amused, through the merchandising of peace by commercial means."

In our materialistic society, Schutz believes Christians should be "a sign of contradiction, living in prayer, joy and communion, in the childlike spirit of Christ."

Roger Schutz's high purpose is to bring Christians of all denominations together in fellowship and love, not only as pilgrims or brothers at the Taizé Community, but in the whole life of the Church. This remarkable French Protestant leader is devoting his life to the unity of God's people, everywhere. He frequently quotes Christ's prayer for his disciples "that they may all be one, that the world may believe." He campaigns tirelessly for ecumenism at every kind of Christian gathering — from Lambeth Palace to the Vatican, from a humble French village to a youth rally at St. Paul's Cathedral.

His dedication to Christian Unity began imperceptibly early in his life. Born in Provence during the First World War, the son of a Swiss Protestant pastor and a French mother, with both parents themselves coming from family traditions of the Reformed ministry, the young Roger knew a family life centred upon a strict Protestant piety — but never exclusively so. He recalls the deep impression made upon him when his father went to pray in a Roman Catholic church. He studied theology at Lausanne, leading Bible studies as president of the Student Christian Federation, and with a few students and friends practised a form of Christian community life. He wrote his thesis on the monastic movement. Somehow, he felt himself increasingly called by God to start Christian community life again within the Protestant churches. Soon it was 1940. . . .

Schutz's vision of a restored Protestant monastic life has come true quite dramatically, though perhaps not in the way he expected. No major Protestant denomination has re-established monasticism within its life. Instead, the Taizé community in a very real sense belongs to all the Churches, Protestant and Catholic. Also, the re-discovery of 'community' is currently happening within the life of the whole Christian Church, with many and varied experiments in Christian community living. The Taizé Community, and the vision of Roger Schutz, have done much to inspire this movement.

Schutz sees Christian Unity as essential for the fulness of the Christian life — but he regards the organisational unity of the Churches as secondary to a radical ecumenism of the Spirit, which spreads out into a Christ-inspired unity for all mankind. A close friend of Pope John XXIII, Roger Schutz and other Taizé brothers worked hard behind the scenes at the Second Vatican Council to reconcile opposing viewpoints. He also supported various schemes for the uniting of Protestant Churches. But, by the late 1960's Schutz had become impatient that the Churches were so slow to come together, and sought another way forward. It was to be the Council of Youth.

This is quite a remarkable phenomenon. It reflects the distinctive spiritual life of Taizé and of Roger Schutz himself. It is not really a movement, and even less an organisation, but rather a "happening in the Spirit," a true adventure in Christian renewal and love for the Church and the world. It has been happening because the youth of many countries from the late 1960s onwards began to make their way to Taizé — sometimes flocking there in huge numbers — and because Prior Schutz determined to listen to them, and to take very seriously their spiritual quest. He wrote: "One winter a few years ago, a group of young people came to Taizé. They spoke of their disappointment with the Church, and of their desire to really know the Risen Christ. And I said to myself 'they will take over where I leave off.' "

1968's revolutionary youth upheavals in Paris and elsewhere faced Roger Schutz and the Taizé Community with the radical demands of a world in ferment, seeking justice. Schutz saw that Taizé had to be open to this radical quest — and this clinched his new understanding of Christian Unity. It had to be the unity of the whole people of God for the whole of mankind. The Church had to become, as never before, a living body serving men and women in their deepest needs. Schutz believed Taizé had to embrace the yearnings and searchings of contemporary youth — so that a real world revolution could be built on the lasting foundations of the Christian hope.

At Easter 1970, 2500 people, mostly teenagers, assembled at Taizé heard the proclamation of the 'Joyful News', heralding the preparation for the Council of Youth: "The Risen Christ comes to quicken a festival in the innermost heart of man. He is preparing a springtime of the Church, a Church devoid of means of power, ready to share with all, a place of visible communion for all humanity. He is going to give us enough imagination and courage to open up a path of reconciliation. He is going to prepare us to give our life so that man may be no longer victim of man."

As more and more young people came to Taizé, Roger Schutz himself preached less, and listened more — often for hours at a stretch. He paid close attention to the hopes and visions of the youth of many nations, from many social and religious backgrounds. In recent years the numbers of young people, indeed people of all ages, flocking to Taizé, have swelled enormously. At Easter 1972, some 16,000 heard the announcement that the Council of Youth would begin in 1974. Early in September 1974, 40,000 flocked to that Church of Reconciliation, in the heart of the Burgundy countryside, for its launching.

During the previous four years, groups of young people right across the world set up prayer cells and 'listening posts' in preparation for the Council. Often they reflected on the injustices of their society — particularly so in Latin America, with its terrible extremes of riches and poverty. Sometimes their letters were read out during worship at Taizé, for the Council of Youth soon came to have within it a world-wide fellowship of prayer.

Once launched, the Council of Youth has spread, imperceptibly, into many parts of the worldwide Church. As Roger Schutz sees it, it is a unique event in the life of the Church — and he is certainly right. It is a means whereby young people from many churches and many lands can contribute to and participate in the renewing of the Church of Christ — but Prior Roger gives a vision, not a blueprint. Each young person, challenged by Taizé, must decide — through prayer and reflection — his or her part in the renewal. Prior Roger knows that if men and women open themselves to God in the very depths of their being, the will of God for their lives will become clear. Such openness is the way of true prayer.

"The man of prayer finds his happiness in continually creating, searching, being with Christ. In our society, where man can slip towards chaos and the law of the jungle if he takes the easy road, we cannot accept that way, but must work for the transformation of society in Christ."

Many Christians, young and old, understand the Council of Youth as a 'festival of joy.' Certainly, for Prior Roger himself, words like 'joy,' 'festival,' 'struggle and contemplation' sum up the essence of true contemporary spirituality, of life in the Risen Christ. His understanding of 'joyful festival' blends mysticism, evangelicalism and radicalism.

"How do you call a festival in the middle of a struggle for justice and liberation? In all men there is an empty heart of loneliness, and there, in that heart of infinite loneliness, which no degree of human intimacy can dispel, Christ is waiting for us, Risen from the dead. In communion with Him, one finds festival, the happiness of God."

Prior Schutz sees our Western society as sick unto death. He sees that we are preoccupied with material concerns, with getting and having, rather than with giving and sharing. We buy and sell pleasure, to conceal and drown our inner restlessness. Our consumer society is spiritually bankrupt. Prior Schutz believes healing can only come 'through struggle and contemplation': the struggle for a just social order, motivated by contemplation upon, and life in, the Risen Christ. Totally devoting his life to the unity of the Church, for the unity of mankind through the way of 'joyful festival' and 'struggle and contemplation,' Roger Schutz of Taizé inspires and challenges the whole Church to the deepest commitment to life in the Risen Christ for the sake of our neighbour, mankind.

Prior Roger Schutz of Taizé: Key facts
Born 1915 in Provence, son of Swiss Pastor and French mother of Reformed (Protestant) background. Studied theology at Lausanne. Became interested in community life as a student. First visited Taizé August 1940. 1940-42: lived at Taizé, praying, and helping Jewish refugees escape to Switzerland. Went to Switzerland, returned to Taizé 1944; community developed. 1949: Easter Sunday: first seven brothers took life vows. 1952 onwards: Taizé 'Fraternities' began to be set up in various parts of the world. Increasingly involvement of Taizé Community, under Prior Roger's leadership, in Ecumenical Movement. Mid-1960's onwards: increasing number of young people drawn to Taizé. 1966: first big international youth meeting at Taizé. 1970: Proclamation of the 'Joyful News,' and preparation for the Council of Youth. 1974: Council of Youth launched. 1976: Roger Schutz goes to Calcutta to meet Mother Theresa. *Books include: The Power of the Provisional, Unity: Man's Tomorrow, Festival, Struggle and Contemplation.*

Renewing the Church

Cardinal Suenens

Cardinal Suenens
Renewing the Church

Outside the Vatican itself, probably few Roman Catholic leaders have greater influence on current developments within the Roman Church in Europe and North America, than Léon Joseph, Cardinal Suenens, the Primate of Belgium and the Archbishop of Malines-Brussels. For well over a decade, he has been a leading advocate of the whole movement of renewal and change following the Second Vatican Council. He has been personally involved in carrying out some of its major reforms. Yet he is certainly no extremist or revolutionary. Indeed, he has been called a churchman of the 'extreme centre': by that, he understands a constructive bringing together of 'past, present and future' in the Church.

To meet him is to be with a quiet person, one with no sense of ecclesiastical pomp and circumstance, a man uniting an efficient, businesslike manner with a very real humility. Strong in his convictions about the Church and its future, his mind and heart remain ever open to the movement of the Spirit. At seventy-three, he looks much younger, and is certainly 'young at heart.' I was both very impressed with the man, and equally fascinated by the very wide range of his Christian concerns — from reforms within the Roman Catholic Church to the Charismatic Movement across all Christian traditions, from evangelism to reach the empty heart of contemporary agnostics and atheists, to the movement of Christian Unity.

Born in 1904 of a poor Brussels family, from an early age he was determined to preach the Gospel and serve the Church. Studies at the Gregorian University in Rome led to religious education work and clergy training: from 1930 to 1940 the young Léon Suenens was Professor of Philosophy at Malines Seminary. During the Second Wold War, he was vice-rector of the famous Catholic university at Louvain. Dealing with the occupying German Army gave him a good schooling in diplomacy, a skill he was subsequently to use most effectively within the Church! From 1945 to 1961, he was Auxiliary Bishop to the Cardinal Archbishop of Malines-Brussels, which latter position he has himself held since 1962. Since then, he has become not only widely known and respected within the Roman Catholic Church, but also highly regarded among Christians of all denominations, for his imaginative approach to the problems facing Christians everywhere, and all the Churches.

A close friend of Pope John XXIII, Cardinal Suenens was a key figure at the Second Vatican Council. His own thinking was very close to that of Pope John. He suggested to him that the Council should be a dialogue within the Church, and between the Church and the world. He was one of the four chairmen at the last three sessions of the Council. He saw the involvement of the Roman Catholic Church in the whole ecumenical movement as both inevitable and desirable: he firmly rejects any notion that Roman Catholics are a closed family. He is deeply committed to the coming together of Catholic and Protestant Christians.

He put it to me this way: "Whatever happened to us that for so many centuries we were so estranged from each other? For centuries, we did not even speak to each other! Now all that is in the past: a new way of feeling ourselves to be Christians together is emerging. To win the battle for the souls of men, all Christians must come together to work for the ultimate aim of full communion in faith."

Suenens dreams of a united Church in the 21st century. "For the first ten centuries, we were one; in the second millennium we were divided; for the third millennium it is my hope we will see one Church again, in a richer unity, but where unity does not mean uniformity, a unity really in depth. That will be for me the dream of my life."

Certainly the Belgian Cardinal practises the ecumenical spirit in his own life and work. On several occasions he has shared the same platform as Michael Ramsey, former Anglican Archbishop of Canterbury, when both have spoken on the need for Christians to work and worship more closely together. He has written a book, jointly with the former Archbishop, on *The Future of the Christian Church*. No stranger to Britain and its churches, preaching engagements in this country have taken him to such varied pulpits as York Minster — and the London School of Economics! When he came over for the all-churches' South-West Ecumenical Congress at Bristol four years ago, he preached in a local Baptist church for the nationwide TV service.

He travels widely in the cause of greater understanding and fellowship between Catholics, Protestants and other Christians. Suenens believes the closer coming together of Christians is essential for mutual growth in the Faith, and for effective evangelism. He stresses that no one section of Christ's Church can experience his renewal in isolation: new life in the Church, and its growing together in unity, go hand in hand. While a keen advocate of reforms in the

Church, particularly the replacement of hierarchical power by shared decision-taking — 'collegiality' — and a much more active role for lay people, Suenens admits that streamlining church organisation can never be enough in itself.

"In the past decade, the institutional reforms in the Church had the most importance in the public eye. Now the time has come to appreciate the more profound element in renewal, the invisible side, the spiritual side."

He looks at secular society, and sees that contemporary man is experiencing a God-shaped vacuum. "Man still has an emptiness to be filled. He has a sheer hunger for God, the someone who knows him from the inside. Man today seeks a true contemplation of God, and longs to rejoice in God's radiant fulness."

Such a need can only be met by Christians as they themselves experience the fulness of the Holy Spirit in their life and faith. From his worldwide travels and contacts with many different Christian movements, both Catholic and Protestant, Suenens believes this is happening, and that ours is 'the time for true charismatic renewal.'

Certainly he sees real hope in the widespread Charismatic movement, as long as it avoids excesses, and as long as its adherents don't claim any superiority over other Christians. Suenens has written an important book, *A New Pentecost?*, about the movement, and has attended great charismatic gatherings both in Europe and in the United States.

"Christ is working today through the Holy Spirit for the evangelical renewal, the pentecostal revival of the Church. I think what is coming and what is badly needed is an increase of spirituality among the Christians of today. Spirituality really means 'Holy Spirit at work,' a profound action of the Holy Spirit in his Church, renewing that Church from the insde." He stressed to me that the Holy Spirit's work of renewing the Church begins in the life of each Christian. "Real Church renewal happens in each of us, for we, after all, are the Church. We are so accustomed to speak of the Church as something outside ourselves, criticising it, saying it should do this or that. We forget that *we are the Church*, all of us together. But too often in the past, our church life has become dead, stifled by the dust of centuries and the burden of tradition. Even today, it is often impersonal."

Every different denomination has its own kind of suffocating dust! So, for the future, the whole style and atmosphere of our parish life must be changed, under the power of the Spirit! In the renewed and revitalised Church of the future, local church life must be characterised by loving, caring, warm fellowship — it must be "the loving parish!"

"Warmth and fraternity are needed in our churches. People reproach us because we are not Christian enough. We must know each other and love each other in our parish life. Prayer, reflection on God's word, and love in action, express the Holy Spirit's work in each of us. Christ is renewing his Church today through the Holy Spirit. The challenge of today to us as Christians is this — will we open ourselves to be possessed by him?"

What does all this mean in terms of practical action? Certainly for Cardinal Suenens it means the Church taking very seriously the issues and problems of secular society, and grappling with them. At the Second Vatican Council, he urged the vital importance of the question of world population explosion and birth control. He believes there must be the fullest possible discussion, within the Roman Catholic Church, about whether priests must be required to be celibate, or whether the marriage of priests can be allowed. Suenens himself favours the ordination of married men to the Roman Catholic priesthood where the numbers of unmarried clergy are inadequate for parish needs. On the question of the organisation of the Roman Catholic Church, and the authority of the Pope, he is a firm advocate of 'collegiality,' the sharing of power between the Pope and the bishops. In this, he continues the outlook of Pope John XXIII, but so far Pope Paul VI has not wanted this to the extent that would mean any real lessening of papal power. Of course Suenens rejects any notion that he is 'attacking the Pope'; rather, he wants its exercise of power and authority to come in line with the democratic spirit of the contemporary age.

As Archbishop of Brussels, the city which is the main focus of the European Economic Community, Cardinal Suenens believes the Churches must take very seriously the challenge of the Common Market. Particularly, he declares that the rich nations of the nine Western European countries of the Community must not become a 'rich man's club,' but must always remember their responsibilities towards the poor — both within Europe, and in the wider world of the developing countries.

"The preaching of the Gospel and its acceptance imply a social revolution whereby the hungry are fed and justice becomes the right of all."

In our personal lives, and in the life of society at all levels, we are called to be liberated through God's Spirit to live a life of love for humanity. Suenens holds this means being liberated from all false ideas about God: "A certain kind of God has now died. That God was remote, a restricting power, over against man, and interfering against man. We rightly reject such false notions of God. For we must not reject man in favour of God, nor reject God in favour of man: we must choose God and man, for the glory of God is man alive, supremely in Christ.''

For Cardinal Suenens, who is very much in the long tradition of great Roman Catholic reforming leaders, and very much a churchman of the 1970s, the Christian must affirm both God and man. The Christian must live in the Church and in the secular world. The work of the Church cannot be left to bishops and priests — it must involve the whole people of God. Hence Cardinal Suenens is such a keen advocate of the education of the laity in both the inner life of the Church, and in the Church's work in society. He stresses that "the idea that the clergy are in charge of the Church is changing more and more. We are all together the Church — laity, priests, nuns, bishops and Pope." He believes the effectiveness of the whole Church of Christ in this secular age largely depends on the quality of the witness of the laity. He is in no doubt that today's world needs — and needs desperately — the effective witness to the Gospel.

When he was awarded the Templeton Prize for Progress in Religion, for 1976, he declared: "The world is sick to death of its atheism. That is the tragedy of our time."

Only the power of the Spirit, through the people of God, can overcome such a sickness. Only Christ's love, flowing into the world through his Church, can renew mankind: "We cannot have a Eucharist without some bread, some wine; we cannot have a baptism without water. So, too, Christ cannot live his life today in this world without our mouth, without our eyes, without our going and coming, without our heart. When we love, it is Christ loving through us. This is Christianity."

Cardinal Suenens: Key facts
Born Brussels 1904. Studied at Gregorian University in Rome. 1930-40: Professor of Philosophy at Malines Seminary. 1940-45: Vice-Rector of Louvain Catholic University. 1945-61: Auxiliary Bishop to the Cardinal Archbishop of Malines-Brussels. 1962 onwards: Cardinal Archbishop of Malines-Brussels, and the Roman Catholic Primate of Belgium. 1962-65: played key role at Second Vatican Council. 1976: Awarded Templeton Prize for Religion. *Books* include: *The Gospel to Every Creature, The Future of the Christian Church, Co-reponsibility in the Church, A New Pentecost?*

With God among the Down-and-Outs

Sally Trench

Sally Trench

With God among the Down-and-Outs

Of all the outstanding Christian people I have ever met, Sally Trench is certainly among the most remarkable and most unusual. Her experience is a unique one; her story one of the most extraordinary of recent times. For five years she devoted herself totally — almost to the point of death — to central London's meths drinkers, dossers and down-and-outs. Her incredible story, which she told in best-selling *Bury Me in My Boots*, brought her overnight fame she had never sought. It also enabled her to begin to do something long-term to prevent youngsters on the streets becoming drop-outs and tramps.
How did it all happen?

As a child and teenager, young Sally was a rebel. Brought up in a wealthy family with all the comforts of life, she instinctively reacted against anything which put money before people. She rejected the shallow materialistic values which she felt all around her. Her upbringing and schooling she found restricting and conformist — and Sally refused to conform!

"The years from seven to seventeen were very unhappy for me," she told me. "I was sent to a very prim and proper boarding school, and totally rebelled against it. I just wouldn't conform, and made myself very awkward with everyone in authority. Eventually I was expelled: the headmistress had no choice, and I don't blame her!" Sally was only fifteen.

Sent back home, she soon went off to Africa to seek adventure, and found more than she had bargained for! "I found myself among game wardens, hunting rhinos, and learning to survive out in the open. I learned then I have a very strong survival instinct! Actually, I walked much of the way, and eventually landed up in Durban."

Returning to England, Sally was at Waterloo Station, and for the first time saw meths drinkers — ragged, dirty, society's throwouts. She immediately felt drawn to them, and drawn to help them to the point of identifying with them. For she herself felt deeply isolated and alienated from society, and at one with its social rejects.

Obliged to stay at home for a year, she often left the house in the middle of the night, climbing down the drainpipe and making her way to central London. There, she visited railway stations and other haunts of meths drinkers and tramps, taking them food, coffee and blankets — "anything I could scrounge!" She discovered a new world — of terrible poverty, degradation, of life at the very lowest level, of men slowly dying through cold, exposure and addiction — and new relationships, too.

"I really enjoyed meeting them and helping them. I didn't set out with any intention of saving them. That concern only came later; it happened by chance. I cared for them — and they cared for me. They smiled; they welcomed me; they were really pleased to see me; they gave me an unconditional affection. It wasn't just a matter of their welcoming me because I brought them food; I accepted them as people, as human beings, and they were not used to that." The down-and-outs accepted Sally, and she wasn't used to that, either! Almost suddenly, it was as if all the rejection and hatred she had previously experienced was replaced by a tremendous sense of love — between people, and, as Sally understands it, from God to herself and others. For, from an early age, she had a very strong sense of the reality and presence of God. She knew that God is for real.

"I recall vividly that at the age of ten, I realised there are only two people in this world I would *have* to live with, from first thing in the morning to last thing at night, and those two people are myself and God. But that's the wrong order! I've been trying ever since then to get the order right!"

As a boarder at the Roman Catholic convent school from which she was eventually expelled, the one thing she accepted unreservedly was commitment to the Christian Faith. "At school, I reacted very well to religion. I was always first in the chapel for Mass! All I had to survive on was God. For many years I had nothing to hang on to, except immense faith. God kept me and held me through those very unhappy years."

One of the many remarkable and very memorable things about meeting Sally Trench, is the easy and quite matter-of-fact way she talks about God being real for her. She doesn't use pious words or the traditional language of the Church. But when she talks about "the warmth of God" and "God's love coming through me and through other people," you know she means it, and it's not just churchy clichés.

Round-the-clock practical action, not Sunday-only piety, is what Christianity means to Sally Trench. Among the dossers and meths drinkers, the tramps and the junkies, she first understood God's total identification with the needs of the poor and forgotten of society, and first grasped the meaning of true Christian compassion for them. She concluded she could not be half-hearted or half-committed about it. It had to be for real — full-time. So, after a year of furtive, nocturnal escapades from her comfortable home in a fashionable part of London to the haunts of the down-and-outs, she finally left home altogether, to devote herself to them completely.

The sheer appalling need of these pathetic people, who desperately wanted someone to care for them but usually had enough pride left not to solicit it, overwhelmed her. "I felt I had to do something about it. The more I worked and lived among them, the more positive I became about it all. It was something that grew, rather than my making a conscious choice."

So began nearly five extraordinary years in Sally's life — life, and sometimes near death, among London's dossers and addicts. She began in earnest. Day after day, week after week, month after month, with little respite except when sheer exhaustion or illness forced her to stop, Sally Trench walked some twenty miles across central London distributing food and drinks among the down-and-outs. From Waterloo and Charing Cross, via Covent Garden, to King's Cross and Euston, and then over to the East end, she tramped the streets, taking provisions and making meals for the dossers, wherever she found them — often in derelict houses or huddled in shop doorways, late at night. Always, she improvised: hers was no social service backed by massive funds! She scrounged food and hot drinks from whatever source she could. Sometimes passers-by, sympathetic to what she was doing, gave her money to buy provisions. As she became known along the Thames Embankment, a favourite area for tramps, the proprietor of a tea-stall there gave her free tea for them. A friendly West End cafeteria saved its left-overs for Sally to take to the tramps. "I used to get all this bread, and other odd items of food, and then take it all to the waiting room at Charing Cross station, where I would sit buttering lots of packs of rolls and sandwiches, filling them with cheese and anything else I could get hold of. People in the waiting-room used to look at me as if they couldn't believe their eyes! Then I would set off to distribute them, all over London."

On many mornings, she scrounged fruit and vegetable left-overs from Covent Garden: Sally's vegetable soup became a favourite in the derelict houses and on the old riverside bombed sites, where many of the tramps lived.

It was a tough life. She lived rough for much of the time, fending for herself as best she could. For most of the time, she had no regular income. She was out in all weathers, often slept on railway stations or out in the open, and not infrequently was up all night. It was a miracle she didn't catch a fatal illness, though she had to go into hospital more than once. What kept Sally going? She certainly had a tough constitution, an iron will, that rare instinct for survival already tested at an early age in the African bush, and an immense determination that what she was doing was right. For through it all, amid all the squalor and exhaustion, was an immense sense of being fulfilled: she had no doubt she was doing God's work.

"I was very close to God when I was doing that," she recalls. "I've always felt close to God, and I certainly feel close to God now, but in those years among the meths drinkers and down-and-outs, the young beats and drug addicts, there was a special dimension to it all. I've never been so close to God before or since, as I was then. I felt that God's love was flowing through me to those people, and that I was receiving his love for me from them, too."

She was not always alone in her work. For several hectic months, she worked as a full-time organiser and social worker for the Simon Community, a new venture in community care for social inadequates launched in the early 1960s by Anton Wallich Clifford. Sally worked closely with him until lack of money forced the closure of several Simon centres, and she decided it was time to revert to her own, highly personal kind of caring. Many of those she was helping had been very hurt by society, and consequently were very suspicious of anything too 'organised' being done for them. They welcomed Sally because she was not 'official,' and didn't ask too many questions. So her work was intensely personal, though she gradually built up a network of friends and families she could call on for help in an emergency — such as offering temporary shelter to a homeless youngster. At places like the Golborne Centre off the Portobello road, a church-run community for tramps, with a few-rules, open-door policy, Sally became a familiar figure — as she did, too, in the coffee bars, pubs and late-night haunts of London's teenage drop-outs.

Sally's life took her among all sorts and conditions of society's rejects. Originally drawn to help meths drinkers and tramps, often middle-aged and old men, she could not ignore the appalling new problem of young addicts and drifters, many in their teens. Often, she spent her days among them, and then, after snatching a few hours' rest, made her nightime rounds of the tramps and crude spirit drinkers, taking them refreshments, and giving them basic medical care. Helping to 'dry out' a young alcoholic, staying close to a junkie while he or she recovered from a 'bad trip' or struggled to break free from the vicious addiction, spending desperate hours with a teenager bent on suicide, or simply sitting around in coffee bars talking plain, Christian common sense with a group of young drop-outs — such was all in a day's work for Sally Trench. Once, she was arrested and searched for being a suspected drug addict herself!

And that night's work could mean holding the hand of a dying tramp, smiling at him to show someone cared, as he coughed away his last pain-wracked hours in this world.

Through all these remarkable experiences, Sally Trench found herself possessed of great depths of courage — physical and spiritual. Once she threw herself into a brawl, separating two junkies fighting with knives. On another occasion, she risked her own life rushing into a burning building to save an old tramp. She had plenty of spiritual courage, too. She never went out of her way to 'preach at' people, believing Faith in action was her calling, but she made no bones about stating the Gospel's claims when the occasion demanded it. The young drug addicts and drop-outs called her "Sally the Christian," with an almost grudging respect — but they knew her Christianity was for real.

Eventually the sheer physical exhaustion and mental strain was too much: Sally Trench had to spend time in a mental hospital. When she had fully recovered, she pondered the next step. "I had got to the stage when I realised the need for a more normal life than the one I was living. I had no normal friends: virtually everyone I knew was a tramp, meths addict, prostitute or junkie. I knew then that unless I had some normality in my life, I really would have a nervous breakdown, and then I would be no use to anyone. I had to have some stability — and that was how the book, *Bury Me in My Boots*, came about. I didn't decide to write a book; I decided, for purely personal reasons of my own sanity, to keep a diary of my daily experiences, a record of life among the down-and-outs. So there I was, at two in the morning every night on Euston station, scribbling away on toilet paper! Eventually, I had written 75,000 words, but I had no thought of publishing it. I kept it in one of the left luggage lockers."

It would have remained a purely personal diary, unknown to the public, had it not been for a tragic incident which proved a turning-point in the life of Sally Trench. One night she was called to the side of a fourteen-year-old girl, who lay dying on a derelict site. "She had tried to carry out an abortion on herself with a knitting needle, and when I reached her there was no hope; she had lost too much blood. She didn't want an ambulance, but her priest — so I brought him to the scene as fast as I could. She died soon afterwards. The priest was absolutely furious with me, as he thought I was a junkie and in some way responsible for the girl's death. When I explained about my life and work among the down-and-outs, he warned that if I wasn't very careful, I would probably end up dead as well. Then I mentioned about my diary, and he became very interested. He asked to read it, and eventually he was responsible for getting it published."

The success of the book was amazing. Overnight it became a best-seller in Britain, and it went on to be published in several other countries, becoming a best-seller in Spain, Norway and elsewhere. The sheer vivid honesty of *Bury Me in My Boots*, and its revelations of life on the very margins of modern society, as experienced by a remarkable young woman, were almost sensational. The book brought Sally Trench fame. The mass media threw the spotlight onto her and her work. Press, TV and radio clamoured for her. She was interviewed on the David Frost programme. She was invited to cocktails with the Queen. From the squalor of life among the forgotten, she was suddenly under the glare of publicity. "I was just amazed by the success of the book, and astonished by it all." Sadly, perhaps inevitably, it meant the end of her work among the dossers.

"They didn't like the fact that I had written a book about them. They could not understand the purpose of it. They felt I had used them for my own ends, and that my concern for them had not been genuine. It was all very sad. I was physically attacked; I might have been killed. So I had to give that work up. It was inevitable, I suppose."

It was the end of one chapter, and proved to be the beginning of another, for Sally Trench.

Five years among drop-outs and old dossers taught Sally Trench the enormous difficulty of 'cure,' and the all-important need for prevention. The most important thing is to prevent people, especially young people, from drifting into aimless street life, drug addiction, alcoholism and petty crime — all or any of which can have tragic consequences in themselves, and can certainly lead into a spiral of personal inadequacy and anti-social behaviour, with a lonely death in a dark doorway as the wretched conclusion.

So this is what Sally Trench is doing now: helping to prevent today's youngsters 'at risk' from becoming the down-and-outs and meths-addicts of tomorrow. She uses her spacious home in north London as a school for truants and problem children from a nearby comprehensive school, under a special project supported by the Inner London Education Authority. They do Maths and English in the morning, and all sorts of activities such as art, drama and modelling, in the afternoon, with occasional outings to places of interest, exhibitions or sports events. The 'school' is run as an informal home, and Sally is helped by a full-time teacher and volunteers. The aim is to restore the children's confidence in themselves and their abilities, and develop their sense of responsibility towards others. It seems to be working: nineteen of the twenty-five who did 'alternative school' at Sally's home in the project's first year, went back to full-time school.

Sally Trench knows such work is neither as dramatic nor as likely to catch the headlines as her former activities among the dossers, but she says quite categorically: "These disadvantaged kids are the drop-outs and meths drinkers of tomorrow — unless we do something to prevent it now. The problem is bigger than truancy. In London and elsewhere, you will find children on the streets at night, their parents out on shift work or at the public house. These children need a proper family life and real caring, as well as the educational side." In Leeds, her Project Spark, of which she is Director, attempts to tackle some of these wider facets of the problem. Disadvantaged children — 'latchkey children' — aged between nine and fifteen, in one of the poorest districts of Leeds, are offered a fun rendezvous and academic help at the Family Evening Centre. Based in an ordinary terraced house, the Centre provides table tennis, boxing, cooking, woodwork, dancing and other activities.

"Perhaps it is significant that in an area where muggings are commonplace and Saturday night knifings a way of life, there has been no thieving, vandalism or graffiti on the walls of what the kids like to call 'our club,' " Sally comments. She is hoping to develop similar projects in other needy areas, if she can raise the necessary finance.

"Project Spark was manifested from a vision and belief that it could help 'disadvantaged' young people. Society has labelled them as 'deprived' or 'maladjusted' or simply as 'drop-outs.' Our goal is not to objectify an individual's personality disorder, but to be involved with youngsters as they work through their difficulties so that they return to society more able to cope with themselves and more responsive to the needs of others."

"I do believe if we block paths leading to their personal development and do not support them, we are guilty of their present name-tags such as 'delinquent.' I have seen such condemnation and isolation lead twelve-year-olds to ill-health, alcoholism, drug abuse, prostitution and so on. It has also been my experience that many kids I have met, who in spite of their problems have great potential and hope for themselves, have been destroyed because our society will not find the time nor resources to fill their needs."

As much now as in her former work among the down-and -outs, Sally Trench keeps close to God, and believes in a very matter-of-fact, yet also very profound way, that it is His work. "God gives me the grace to do it, through His Spirit, and with His love. But I don't push religion among the children here at day-school. There is a cross on the mantlepiece, and they can ask about religion as they want to. We often have Mass here, and nuns and priests drop in and help us; the example is the most important thing for the children. I want them to see religion in action."

Sally Trench's challenge to us, as a very courageous and imaginative Christian, is quite simply this — to put our religion into action! She challenges society to realise its responsibilities towards those it can so easily reject and forget. God is very real for Sally, and because of that, she gets things done. As she puts it so simply — "I do have this very strong sense of the reality of God. He has made me a whole person, in that He has taken hold of me and done things with me and through me."

Sally Trench: Key facts
Born 1945; left boarding school when fifteen; travelled to Africa; worked among dossers and drug addicts in London — 1963-68; wrote best-selling book, *Bury Me in My Boots* (published 1968); wrote *Jake,* a pamphlet about meths drinkers; 1971 — began Project Spark in Leeds; 1975 — extended Project Spark to London. She has worked with Anton Clifford in the Simon Community, studied social science, and written articles on drug addiction and alcoholism.

Break down the walls that separate

Pauline Webb

Pauline Webb

Break Down the Walls that Separate

There are more women than men in the world today. There are certainly more women than men in the Churches. Yet, oddly enough, very few women hold key positions in the life and work of the Churches, and so the key decisions, affecting men and women, are usually taken by men.

Someone who is an exception to this is Pauline Webb, one of the leading figures of the Methodist Church in Britain, who is also known worldwide for her devotion to the global Christian fellowship in her work for the World Council of Churches. She certainly sees campaigning for a fairer deal for women, inside and outside the Church, as a vital expression of her Christian discipleship. As the first woman to hold office in the World Council — she is former Vice-Moderator of its Central Committee — she has thought a great deal about Christian faith in relation to women's rights.

"The WCC is primarily concerned with the proclamation of the wholeness of the Gospel — the Gospel that is good news for all — the news that God created us all, male and female, in the divine image; that the Saviour came to offer us all, men and women, a full, abundant human life; that the Spirit brings into being among us all a new community where Jew and Greek, bond and free, male and female, are one in Jesus Christ."

"That's the good news and yet so much of our experience in the world today denies that reality. The image of God is defaced whenever people devalue one another on grounds of race or class or sex; the new life in Christ is dehumanised whenever people depersonalise and prevent each other from realising their full potentiality; the new community is distorted whenever the diversity of God's creation is turned into the disunity of human sin. Whenever Christians find anything which distorts the Christian Gospel and defies God's purposes, their duty is to expose it and to end it. That must include any kind of discrimination or subordination or devaluing of a person or group solely on grounds of sex."

Pauline Webb believes Christians, both men and women, must probe deeply into this question if a full understanding of the proper equality of the sexes is to be reached. It's not just a matter of equal opportunity for jobs and equality before the law. Nor is it enough to rejoice in the God-given differences between men and women, and leave it at that. "It's a matter of recognising that alongside these differences there has been a different history, different expectations, a different sense of identity, and a different association with the structures of power, that has created a male-dominated order in almost all human society and certainly within the Church, making it impossible for the Church to foreshadow a truly human community," says Pauline Webb.

Fired by the conviction that women should be much more active at all levels of the Churches' life, including leadership positions, Pauline Webb has demonstrated in her own career this is both feasible and beneficial to the whole Church. A Twickenham schoolteacher of English and Religious Education who became Editor of the Methodist Missionary Society and an 'Ecumenical Fellow' in Advanced Religious Studies at New York's famous Union Theological Seminary, she was elected Vice-President of the Methodist Conference in 1965, and for six years was Director of Lay Training for the whole Methodist Church in Britain. Since 1973 she has held one of the key posts in the Nonconformist Churches — as Executive Secretary of the Overseas Division of the Methodist Church, with special responsibilities for links with the autonomous Methodist Churches in West Africa and the Caribbean. She also holds a focal role in ecumenical life in Britain, as Chairman of the British Council of Churches' Community and Race Relations Unit. On the global Church scale, she is on the WCC Central Committee, and currently is the only British member of its Executive Committee, having previously spent five years as a Commissioner of the WCC Anti-Racism Programme.

Of course, she would never say it herself, but her own life shows that women can be leaders within the Christian Church!

I talked with her about the question of women's role in the Church. Her views are undoubtedly controversial, but also undoubtedly reflect those of a growing number of women throughout the world's Churches. "There is discrimination against women in the Churches, though it is not usually recognised or acknowledged as such. Leadership in church organisations, except in women's work, is exercised almost exclusively by men; this is usually regarded as quite normal and is only now beginning to be questioned. Many committees and councils of the Churches are made up entirely or largely of men. Women have special qualities to bring to Christian committee work — we tend to personalise issues rather than generalise. We ask 'what does this mean to people?' whereas men approach problems in a more abstract way. Both approaches are necessary, which is why men and women must work together in partnership for the Church."

"I think that attention to detail — very important in church work — is more a female characteristic than a male one. And women have more sensitivity to what is happening between people, underneath the argument, which is also very important. No committee is a human community without both men and women."

"Christianity is an emancipating faith. It brings liberation through the Gospel in faith and action. But the Christian Church, as an institution, has not been a sufficiently liberating institution for women, in the sense of not opening up to them the full range of possibilities."

Because Christian theology, down the centuries, has been almost entirely written by men, the religious insights of women have perhaps been neglected. Pauline Webb puts this point quite strongly:

"The whole way we present and think about the Christian faith is very much in male terms. In theology, for example, we naturally think of God as being male. Preaching, too, reflects predominantly male experience. Preachers usually talk about the sins which are more likely to be male sins — pride, for example, which is not usually a female sin. Women are usually too submissive: their 'sin' is that they are not assertive enough! Unfortunately, the Church has too often emphasised submissiveness as a virtue, confusing it with humility. Love involves assertiveness and not only submissiveness."

In society and in the Church alike, discrimination against women has its roots deep in the past, she explained. "In primitive times, religion deemed women 'unclean' and 'unholy', and all the primitive fears and superstitions about women have gone deep into society's unconscious, and into that of the Churches, affecting our behaviour and attitudes even when we are unaware of it. In discriminating against women, the Church has been reflecting social conditions rather than being in the forefront of movements to change them . Equality for women does not mean pretending that men and women are the same, but that both must be allowed to be fully themselves and thus to complement each other."

In short, the 'fair deal' that Pauline Webb pleads for, isn't just a matter of more women on Church committees and holding more key positions, but of men and women sharing together fully in all the Church's activities — "partnership for the sake of the whole Church." She wants a fairer deal for women at all levels of society, too, from the peasant woman in Africa or Asia who may have to walk several miles daily to fetch water for her family, to the young professional girl in Britain who wants equal job opportunities to her male colleagues.

Pauline Webb is committed to bringing Christians together. Although a strong Methodist, she gives high priority to advancing the Ecumenical Movement. She has done much to bring Mehodists and Catholics, Anglicans and Free Church Christians together, not only through her work for the World Council of Churches, but in all kinds of ways. At week of Prayer for Christian Unity meetings, ecumenical all-night vigils in modern churches and ancient cathedrals alike, student gatherings at universities and colleges, and get-togethers in local churches and parishes, Pauline Webb campaigns for Christians to go beyond their differences and divisions, to experience a new unity in serving Christ and advancing His Kingdom among men. She has written Church pageants, religious film and TV scripts, and penned a number of books, about the challenge and excitement of being a Christian in today's world, and the historic development of the Ecumenical Movement in our time.

"We need the enrichment of every ecumenical, inter-racial, cross-cultural encounter that comes our way, and thank God we live in an age where such opportunities of ventures in fellowship are becoming more frequent. And we need beyond that to identify more fully and with deeper commitment with the struggles of all who are seeking to abolish the boundaries of race, sex, class, cultural differences and denominational divisions, in our persistent search for that universal unity which is surely God's will not only for His Church but for the whole human family. So another sign of the Kingdom seen in the life of the Church today is, I believe, the growth of the whole ecumenical movement, in all its manifestations at local, national and international levels, a movement whose constant prayer must be those words which became the theme song of the Nairobi World Council of Churches Assembly, 'Break down the walls that separate us and unite us in a single body.' It is only as we are obedient to our Lord's prayer that we may be one, that we can hope to be a sign that will enable the whole world to believe, not only in the unity of the Church but in the unity of mankind."

She believes we in Britain can learn a lot from Christians overseas, especially from those in the new nations of the Third World. She particularly thinks we can learn from the vitality of their worship — and I've heard her burst into song, with that Nairobi theme hymn *Break down the Walls* and get a congregation really going in really lively fashion, African-church style!

The Ecumenical Movement is not only for the Church, she

emphasises: it means working for the whole world to live as one human family. Both within the ecumenical fellowship of the world's Churches, and within the wider community of the peoples of mankind, we must learn to live truly as a family, to fulfil God's promise for the whole of His Creation. In our world of dwindling natural resources, and terrible inequality between rich and poor nations, that must mean a simpler life-style, Pauline Webb often stresses. 'Live simply that others may simply live,' is a favourite and telling slogan.

"It is no longer a question of economic growth in the developed countries in order that we can share some of our surplus wealth with the under-developed nations. The need now is for a clear cut-back in our usage of oil, food and other commodities, if the world is to survive. We must live simply, that others may simply live. We must re-think our priorities, and strip down our life-style to be a witness to true Christian living at this time."

"Every Christian can play his or her part in this. We can all make a definite commitment to a simpler life-style, by such methods as eating one meal less each week, giving up one luxury each month, reducing holiday spending and cutting personal expenditure and allocating more to mission and develpment giving."

Lively and amusing to meet, with a fund of traveller's tales about the world Church, Pauline Webb is an energetic woman with a message for the Churches today. Speaking from an extraordinarily wide experience of the Ecumenical Movement and mission in the Third World nations, she deserves to be listened to. She is a prophet (or should I say pro-phetess?) with a simple yet tough challenge, to 'break down the barriers' dividing people, Churches and nations.

Pauline Webb: Key facts
Daughter of a Methodist minister. Educated London University and Union Theological Seminary, New York. 1952-54: Member of Education Department of Methodist Missionary Society. 1954-64: Editor of Methodist Missionary Society. 1964-5: Ecumenical Fellow in Advanced Religious Studies at Union Theological Seminary, New York. 1965-66: Vice-President of the Methodist Conference. 1967-73: Director of Lay Training in the Methodist Church. From 1973: Executive Secretary of the Overseas Division of the Methodist Church, responsible for relations with the autonomous Methodist Churches in West Africa and the Caribbean. *Ecumenical*: 1968: Elected Vice-Chairman of the Central Committee of the World Council of Churches at Uppsala Assembly. and held this office until Nairobi Assembly 1975. 1970-75: Commissioner of the WCC Programme to Combat Racism. 1975 onwards: Member of WCC Central and Executive committees. *Books include: Women of Our Company, Women of Our Time, Operation Healing, Are We Yet Alive?, Agenda for the Churches, Salvation Today.*

Voice of Namibia

Bishop Colin Winter

Bishop Colin Winter

Voice of Namibia

In almost bewildering succession, the world's crises flash across the headlines and burst onto our TV screens. Chile, Northern Ireland, South Africa, Lebanon — the atlas of upheaval and suffering seems endless. We are tempted to forget those whose suffering continues after the headlines have turned elsewhere.

Namibia, in southern Africa, is a place whose people we should never forget. Perhaps you know it by the old name of South West Africa. Until 1966 the legal ruler was the South African government, given authority over the country's half a million Black Africans and tiny white community by the United Nations' "mandate", originating with th former League of Nations after the First World War. When South Africa extended its apartheid racialist policies into Namibia, the UN withdrew the mandate — but the South African regime defied the UN and world opinion, and remains in illegal occupation of Namibia to this day. In spite of international pressure, the Namibians' right to freedom has been ruthlessly suppressed, so they are engaged in a major struggle to be free.

One white Englishman has dedicated his life to the Namibian people. He is determined the world shall not forget them, and he devotes himself to being "the voice of the voiceless." He is not a politician — but a priest of the Church of England. Yet the Rt. Rev. Colin O'Brien Winter, Bishop of Damaraland-"in exile", is no ordinary priest or churchman, but truly a Christian prophet of our time.

Deported five years ago for his outspoken and uncompromising opposition to the South African racialist practices against the Black African people of his diocese, Colin Winter since then has devoted his life to their freedom struggle. He campaigns across the world for their cause, speaking at the United Nations, lobbying national parliaments, preaching in huge cathedrals and tiny chapels, and addressing every kind of Christian gathering from youth vigils to peace conferences. Yet he never sought the mantle of Christian exile and freedom advocate — it was thrust upon him. A well-built man in his late forties, to meet him and talk with him is soon to be aware of his deep passion for social justice, and his strong sense of mission as a pastor of his Namibian flock.

An Anglican curate on a housing estate in Eastbourne, in 1959 he was invited by the late Bishop Joost de Blank (another famous Christian name in the anti-apartheid struggle) to serve as rector in a parish at Simonstown in South Africa. In his five years there, he brought about the racial integration of his congregation, and started the first inter-racial youth camps in the Capetown diocese. Then, in 1964, he was appointed Dean of St. George's Cathedral, at Windhoek in Namibia, in the Damaraland diocese. There Colin Winter found the racial situation far worse than he had ever expected, as he told me.

"The situation in Namibia is much worse than in South Africa itself; the racial division is much sharper. There is virtually no white 'liberal' opinion. I was physically and mentally shocked by the violence I witnessed and experienced against the black people in that land. For speaking up for themselves, or going on strike, Africans have been mown down when coming out of church, imprisoned and tortured. Many of them have been church members personally known to me. The Black Africans of Namibia are, for the most part, a deeply Christian people."

Bishop Winter points out that Namibia is enormously rich, with vast deposits of diamonds, copper and uranium, yet many blacks earn only 75p a week. The contract labour system breaks up families and drives men to alcoholism.

"I found the Church there had become virtually a rich club of white racists, with all the power in their hands. There was absolutely no contact between the black and white races. I knew that would have to change — the Church is the only place there where the races have any chance of coming together. I saw this a pastoral responsibility, not something political. I'm primarily a pastor, and certainly not a politician. My first job was to love them, blacks and whites alike, but it proved virtually impossible to bring them together socially."

Community action programmes to help the Black Africans proved very difficult to launch: when Bishop Winter set up feeding schemes and night schools, very few white people in his congregation openly helped — "though some gave money to help almost secretly, while declining to support the projects in public." When he brought Black Christians by bus to Windhoek Cathedral from the outlying rural areas, he encountered violent opposition from the white community. "All sorts of threats were made against me. Many just stayed away from church. A few stayed loyal, but didn't agree with me, so it proved impossible to get a church action programme going to help the Blacks."

"The white people there are totally indifferent to the conditions under which black people are forced to live. Any contact with them is seen as political: to give a cup of cold water to a black in Namibia is a political action. Indeed, most white people in Namibia just don't know how much the blacks suffer."

For seven years, Colin Winter had the vision of setting up an ecumenical centre in Windhoek, open to blacks and whites alike. "It was to be a place where the blacks could go and get a meal, have a cup of tea, use a toilet, and somewhere just to sit down. I know it sounds incredible, but there is nowhere in Windhoek for a black African to do any of these things!"

He raised 165,000 dollars from the Lutheran World Federation for the scheme, had all the plans drawn up — but the local white community vetoed it. His dream of the Christian Centre faded in the nightmare of racial intolerance.

Bishop Winter emphasises the vital Christian Faith of the black people of Namibia. "The Damaraland diocese is 85% black. Ovamboland, the largest tribal area, is strongly Christian." When Bishop Robert Mize was deported in 1968, the elective assembly of the Diocese of Damaraland (a diocese roughly equal in size to France and Italy!), representing Namibia's Anglicans, elected Colin Winter as their bishop. Over the next four years, his increasingly strong commitment to the Africans' struggle, and especially his defence of the Ovambo people against oppression, brought him into ever deeper conflict with the occupying South Africa authorities. The climax was his deportation in 1972, for his part in defending the Ovambo strikers against the exploitation of the contract labour system. Since then, he has been debarred from entering Namibia as well as from returning to South Africa.

Bishop Winter recounts those events: "The deportation order was not a failure of the Church, but a triumph: the regime could not bear the exposure of the truth. The truth is quite simply this — in Namibia, the majority African population are denied the right to vote, to live where they please, to move freely within their own country, and to equal opportunities in education or work. In all the territories controlled by South Africa, the black workers are denied the right to strike or to engage in free collective bargaining. Despite all these restrictions, in December 1971 some twenty thousand Namibian workers staged a massive strike against the contract labour system and against South Africa's illegal occupation. In the face of police brutality and intimidation, and even though they had no other livelihood, they stayed out. By January 1972 it had become a mass movement, with support from the

Churches and many groups throughout the world. The government made token concessions, but in essentials the system remains unchanged. In the police terrorism after the strike, many Africans were imprisoned and killed. Many of them were Church leaders. It is the Black Christians who have been in the forefront of the struggle for basic human rights, and it is they who have suffered."

"For most Africans, the struggle is a non-violent one. They see that as the Christian way. But we should not be surprised if some, through frustration, and seeing there is no chance of real dialogue with the white authorities, finally turn to armed struggle and guerilla warfare."

In 1975, Bishop Richard Wood, suffragan bishop of Damaraland, was also deported — the third Anglican bishop forced to leave Namibia within seven years. With Bishop Wood, Colin Winter travelled to newly-independent Angola, and to its frontier with Namibia, to meet Anglican clergy and many Black Christians who crossed from Namibia to share in worship and conferences. On one occasion, Bishop Winter conducted a Holy Communion service under the trees, with the participants guarded by African freedon fighters, their guns pointed outwards against a surprise South African attack.

"The Churches in Namibia, especially Anglicans and Lutherans, have found a new unity in acting together on real issues, such as the stopping of floggings, instead of just talking about ecumenism. The Church has shown it is not prepared to allow the dehumanisation of people by intimidation and torture. No true Church of the gospel can exist without making its voice heard."

From his meetings with Namibian Christians in Angola and elsewhere, Bishop Winter is certain "a Battle of Britain spirit" now inspires the Christian people of Namibia in their freedom struggle. Many support the South-West Africa People's Organisation — SWAPO — in its liberation movements. "Namibia now is a nation at a unique moment of destiny — as Britain was in 1940. There is a total determination to be free. So many of the young pople, boys and girls alike, have gone through their hour of decision, and have decided death is preferable to slavery. It's an incredible fact — and the great majority of them are Christians, taught in mission schools. When I left Namibia five years ago, I knew that one day it would be liberated, but I didn't know when or how. The changes in Mozambique and Angola, and the new spirit among the young Namibians, and many older ones, too, make me full of hope it will come soon."

Colin Winter remains the Bishop of Damaraland, 'in exile', at the request of the people of his diocese. They have voted overwhelmingly to keep him as their bishop, for they want him to return — when they are free. In the meantime, they are happy for him to be their voice to the conscience of the world. He is more than a voice, of course. He organises fund-raising for the relief of those in distress in his diocese, and arranges scholarships for black doctors to train in Britain. Working from Britain as his base now, the Bishop has established two centres to receive any who have suffered from racial persecution in southern Africa, including Namibian students studying in the country and others who wish to learn about the freedom struggle in southern Africa. The Namibia International Peace Centre, based in the Abbey at Sutton Courtenay in Oxfordshire, offers a home for a number of Namibian and Zimbabwean students. A second centre, Herman jo Toivo House, was opened in London to offer accommodation and a social centre for Namibians studying in Britain and others from Third World countries.

Colin Winter also gives voice to the voiceless people of Namibia through his books, such as *Just People* and *The Desert in Chains*, telling of the sorrows and joys of the Black Christians in southern Africa today.

A fundamental theological issue is behind the racial crisis in southern Africa, Bishop Winter believes. "In the past, Christians had to defend the doctrine of God. In South Africa today, the doctrine of man is being attacked by the apartheid system. Yet South Africa prides itself on its high rate of churchgoing, so there could be no apartheid today if the Churches had upheld the doctrine of man."

Freedom in southern Africa, and the whole question of race, is a "tremendous challenge to the churches of Britain" affirms Bishop Winter, because "there can be no true Gospel without liberation, and no proper Christian mission without freedom." Investment and economic support from Western countries, particularly Britain, help South Africa maintain apartheid and entrench its illegal hold over Namibia. "Namibia is being looted," Bishop Winter frankly comments. "Major British and Western firms have considerable investments in Namibia, but these investments are not geared to developing the economy of the country and the enrichment of its people. The profits are being repatriated to foreign shareholders or used to reinforce the oppression system. Namibia desperately needs economic development to benefit its own people. The Churches in Britain have a special responsibility to stand with their fellow Christians of Namibia in their freedom struggle, and to press the British government to support inter-national action through the United Nations to bring freedom to Namibia."

Bishop Colin Winter is a prophet — and prophets are not universally popular! In southern Africa he faced open hostility; in Britain, it is often sheer indifference. The note of prophetic utterance has faltered in our Church life. Colin Winter is sounding it again, loud and clear, both internationally and to British Christians. Will we heed him, the 'voice for the voiceless?'

Bishop Colin Winter: Key facts
Born Stoke-on-Trent 1928. Educated Loughborough College, Oxford University and Ely Theological College. Ordained Church of England deacon 1956 and priest 1957, in Chichester diocese. Convinced Christian pacifist. 1956-59: curate at Eastbourne. 1959-64: rector of the parish church of Simonstown, near Capetown, South Africa. 1964-68: Dean of St. George's Cathedral, Windhoek, Namibia. 1968: elected Bishop of Damaraland. Became identified with Namibian human rights and freedom struggle. Deported by South African occupying regime in 1972, after Ovambo workers' strike. Since 1972 has been 'Bishop of Damaraland-in-exile,' with Namibia Peace Centre in Oxfordshire as his base. Campaigns worldwide for Namibia. *Books include: Just People, The Desert in Chains, For George and John.*

Sharing Christ's Passion in Chile

Sheila Cassidy

Sheila Cassidy

Sharing Christ's Passion in Chile

Doctor Sheila Cassidy never set out to be a heroine when she went to Chile in 1971. Indeed, her motives for going to that country were quite undramatic, and, in her own words, even somewhat selfish: "I went neither as a Missionary nor because I was interested in Chile's newly-elected Marxist government, but because, weary of long hours in the National Health Service, I thought I might find life in Chile more pleasant." Of course, she wanted to serve its people with her medical talent — but she also wanted career advancement. Chile seemed to offer that.

Events worked out very differently — it certainly was not the 'easy life!' After two years as a resident doctor in a Santiago teaching hospital, she joined the surgical team at a busy emergency hospital in the city's slums. The poverty of the people, and the sheer inadequacy of what she could do, tore her soul apart. "It was harassing work. I saw one patient every three or four minutes. Though I could diagnose their illnesses, often I didn't have the wherewithall to treat them, for there were no drugs, such as antibiotics, for them to take away. The majority of patients didn't have any money. I felt it was all so wrong. Eventually, I solved the problem to some extent by getting one of the Catholic missionary orders to give me lots of essential drugs, which I gave away to the patients who had no money."

Soon, Sheila Cassidy became aware of even greater poverty, even more desperate need. "My other work was very different, in a very tiny clinic run by the church, in a little wooden building in a shanty town area. I was squashed into one minute room, where I met people much poorer even than those who came to the big hospital. These people were eating only on alternate days; they didn't have even the bus fare to get to the hospital; and they were very desperate people, because they were hungry, because unemployed, because their relatives were in prison, because for them things were only getting worse and worse. They were people with no prospects and no hope. So I had to tackle their anguish, and the only thing I could comfort them with was religion. For the very first time I began to bring my religion actively into my work as a doctor, and I found that talking about God in my work happened naturally. I developed a mixture of counselling and listening, of love and common sense and psychotherapy: this was a way I could help them."

The poor of the slums and shanty shacks of Chile had briefly looked to President Allende's democratic Marxist government for progress and social justice, but the savage military coup had shattered that dream. Under the new regime, oppression and torture became systematised. Because of one act of practical compassion, Sheila Cassidy found herself caught in that web of violence and horror, from which she was fortunate to escape alive. The incident occurred naturally in the course of her dedication to the relief of suffering, irrespective of persons; it was to mark the turning-point of her life.

In November 1975, she was asked to treat a wounded left-wing revolutionary who was on the run from the secret police, and hiding in the house of a group of North American nuns. She operated on his leg, and urged upon the nuns the necessity for adequate medical attention for the man. A few days later, while treating a sick nun, Sheila Cassidy was arrested by armed plain-clothes police, taken to an interrogation centre, and tortured with electrical shocks. Then she was put in solitary confinement for three weeks, and subsequently held in a detention camp for a further five weeks.

After strong diplomatic pressure by the British government, she was eventually released by the Chilean military regime on 29 December, expelled from the country, and returned to Britain. "Suddenly, I found myself transported from the world of torture and solitary confinement to the world of mass media, of radio and television studios, of lectures to packed audiences." The case of Sheila Cassidy brought to the attention of the world, as nothing else had done, the violation of human rights in Chile. Her voice, sounding forth from pulpit and public platform, and re-echoed by the broadcasting media and the press, became the voice for the silent, oppressed peoples of much of Latin America. Indeed, her testimony highlighted the plight of prisoners of conscience in many parts of the globe. Yet Sheila Cassidy has never spoken for any partisan political cause, confining her campaigning to such bodies as the United Nations, Amnesty International, organisations for human rights in Chile, and Church meetings. All over Britain, and in several other countries including the United States, Switzerland and Scandinavia, audiences have responded to her warm, outgoing personality, her effective oratory, her obvious dedication to God and His Church.

For Sheila Cassidy's story is not only one of remarkable courage in a desperate situation, but also one of a woman of strong Christian faith wrestling to give herself totally to God, at whatever the cost.

Born in Lincolnshire in 1937, Sheila Cassidy went with her family to live on a farm in Australia when she was ten years old. The Roman Catholic faith was important to her as a child, as she recalls. "My father was a very ardent Catholic, and my mother was a convert but practised little, though she was a believing Christian. Religion was relatively important for me as a child. I was educated by the Sisters of Mercy, and was enormously impressed by the nuns who taught me: I found it was God that made them tick, and they were people who had given their lives up to God. In my final year at school, I underwent some kind of conversion experience."

"I felt called to a life of total and utter commitment to God, which I interpreted at that time, as I do now, as a call to the religious life — and I was very deeply anguished about it because I didn't want to become a nun and yet I felt this very powerful call."

"By this time I was going to Mass every day and praying a certain amount: even as a child of eight, I had a very strong sense of being at home with God, and a very deep awareness that religion should be a part of daily life and not just for Sunday. I liked to go to church in my everyday clothes!"

When she was fifteen, Sheila Cassidy decided on a career in medicine — "from the moment I made that decision, I never had any desire to do anything else." It was a truly idealistic choice: she wanted to commit herself to the healing of the sick. But she admits to having "hero-worshipped our family doctor!"

University in Australia, and then at Oxford, was followed by clinical training at the famous Radcliffe Infirmary in that city, where in 1963 she qualified as a doctor. Training in plastic surgery, supervision of a casualty department at a Leicester hospital and then the need for more experience in the operating theatre, pointed to a spell overseas. So Sheila Cassidy made the first of her fateful decisions: to go to Chile.

When Allende's government was overthrown and the military dictatorship seized power amid bombing and fighting in Chile's capital of Santiago — where Sheila Cassidy was at the time — she made her second fateful decision: to stay. "What is important to understand is that merely going on living in Chile, I knew that this in itself would involve risk, because by being a doctor in a country where people are continually being wounded and on the run, I knew the moment would come when I would be asked to treat such a person. So, my decision to actually stay in Chile was tantamount to a decision to treat somebody when the moment came."

So when that moment came, in November 1975, Sheila Cassidy's third fateful decision — to treat the wounded revolutionary — had already been taken, at least in principle. Yet, even at that very moment, confronted by a man with a festering, bullet-torn leg, the temptation to refuse, and the fear for her own life, had to be sternly confronted.

"I didn't think twice about helping him, because treating the sick is part of my normal work, whatever the circumstances, but I knew perfectly well it might endanger my own life. I didn't in actual fact think I would be tortured. I thought it possible I might be discovered, interrogated and expelled from the country within twenty-four hours, or I might be killed accidentally in a confrontation. I didn't anticipate the torture: if I had done, I couldn't tell you what my reaction would have been."

Amid the terrible pain and the lonely horror of the torture room, the dark isolation and brooding fears of solitary confinement, and the daily deprivations of prison life, Sheila Cassidy believed herself "very close to death for a good deal of this time," yet, miraculously, was also very close to God. "This period of suffering, loneliness and extreme fear was for me a profoundly religious experience, which had a lasting effect upon my whole attitude to life. While I would never have chosen to suffer in this way, I now count myself greatly privileged to have shared in the anguish of the oppressed peoples of the world and to have participated in some mysterious way in the continuing passion of Christ."

In a strange and profound way, at this moment of extremity of suffering and danger of death, Sheila Cassidy felt herself to be with Christ in His suffering for mankind. "I remember, during the time that I was spread-eagled, stretched out unclothed on the bed being tortured, and in very great pain, that I had a sense of just *being there*, of being present at Christ's passion, as a participant rather than a spectator. It was not the sort of feeling one gets when one tries to meditate on the passion of Christ, which is like being a bystander, and watching someone else suffer and being sorry for them. I just had a very matter-of-fact feeling that I was there, suffering with Him, and that I was no longer a bystander."

"I never felt that God had abandoned me but neither did I feel any particular comfort from His presence — I just knew that He was there, with me, during this time. When one is in very great pain and fear it is extremely difficult to pray coherently, and I could only raise my mind in anguish to God and ask for strength to hold on. I think that my situation, although a rather special one, is comparable with the experience of many people who are helpless and in pain: it is no time for long speeches but for desperately gripping the hand of God."

"Now, as I think in retrospect about this participation in the passion and suffering of Christ, and try to understand it at the intellectual and theological level, I see that because Christ goes on living in us, in everybody, He goes on suffering in us. So in a very real way, in the unmerited sufferings of people throughout the world — for me, particularly vivid with the political prisoners — Christ goes on suffering His Passion, and in the people being tortured, beaten, spat upon, humiliated, everywhere, His passion goes on. In unmerited suffering of this sort, particularly suffering for one's belief, one is really taking part in Christ's redemptive work."

Was this all some kind of mystical experience? Sheila Cassidy herself prefers not to describe it like that, but rather as being with God in the depths of suffering, and struggling to accept His will, whatever happened. "It was a profoundly religious experience; the time in solitary confinement was very important to me. Completely alone in a small cell I knew that I must pray. My first reaction was to pray to be released, and then I realised that within this situation of deprivation there remained to me one liberty: I could ask to be reprieved or I could try to accept whatever God chose to send me. On the night before my trial I believed it was very likely I would be sentenced to several years of imprisonment or even to death, and I fought a long and terrible battle to accept whatever was to happen to me."

"This struggle was to a lesser extent continued during the weeks of my time alone, and many times in the same day I would weaken and pray to be spared further suffering and then, acutely conscious of having withdrawn my gift, apologised and forced myself to say 'Not my will, but Thine be done.' The eventual achievement of the unconditional acceptance of whatever God chose to send me brought a sense of peace and joy which was beyond anything that I had ever experienced. If we can come to want only what God wants, then we are in a curious way untouchable, for then loss of property, of good name, of health, or even of life hold no fears, for if that is what God wants, then we will be at peace."

"This abandonment to the will of God does not come easily, and it must be lived out on a day to day, and minute to minute basis. If we can achieve it, however, we can retain joy and serenity in all manner of pain and adversity, and the courage to face whatever may be."

The struggle of soul and will Sheila Cassidy experienced in the lonely prison cell in Chile, has had a lasting effect on her life — "I try to live *abandoned* to the will of God in little things and in big things, striving with every fibre of my being to want only what He wants, and to allow

Him to be free to do whatever He wants, whether it be successes or failures. This makes it possible for me to be much less vulnerable than I was before, when I cared much more about what people thought and said and my safety."

During her time in prison cramped with other prisoners in crowded conditions, Sheila Cassidy shared her faith with them, Marxists and unbelievers alike, strengthening them as they, too, did their best to care for her after her ordeal of torture. She had held out under terrible pain and fierce cross-examination for twelve hours. She had protected as best she could, the brave nuns and priests who had given shelter to the wounded revolutionary. Incredibly, she felt no antagonism towards her captors and torturers: "I felt sorry for them. I never hated them. for they were the real slaves — slaves to the system, and to their own hatred. Although we prisoners were their captives and victims, we were the truly free ones, because they could not enslave our spirits." Freedom through total acceptance of God's will — that is Sheila Cassidy's challenge. For her, it is no acceptance that comes through blind fatalism, or iron will without love, or suppression of her true self in grim fashion. For to meet her is to meet someone who is obviously very happy, who is in love with life, who bubbles with vitality. It makes you feel good to be with her! Her boyish face bursts with smiles; her holiness is infectiously human.

Most Christians in Britain normally are not faced by such desperate situations as Sheila Cassidy knew in Chile. Ours is the humdrum but necessary task of knowing and serving God in the ordinary, everyday world of school and office, factory and home. She believes prayer is the key to this. "It all comes down to prayer — being faithful to prayer when it's boring and when it's dry just as when it's easy is the absolute keystone to getting to know God. Only as one gets to know him does one have any desire to give oneself to Him, any real desire to change one's life. So, for the vast majority of people, fidelity in commitment to God comes through prayer and fidelity to serving man. Knowing God in serving people is not enough: one can be a very wonderful social worker or doctor, and come very close to God in that, but not as close as when one combines this kind of service with a direct communication with God."

During her experiences in Chile, Sheila Cassidy decided to become a nun. Her conviction to enter the religious life was strengthened during her suffering, reinforcing the power of her Christian witness in a desperate situation. Now that situation is in the past, and the spotlight of mass media publicity has dimmed, she is devoting herself to prayer and study, in preparation for the religious vocation. It does not mean she is rejecting life — the very reverse. Life is at its fullest in serving others and serving God, she stresses, and that's a challenge especially to all young people deciding what to do with their lives.

"The young can discover enormous joy in the service of other people. If they can become outward-looking, and choose careers of service such as medicine, nursing and social work, they will find an untold happiness. Riches and pleasure are as nothing compared with the joy that comes from giving. We are all searching for happiness — and I'm convinced one finds this in the service of man and God."

"This immense secret I long to share with people: don't think of yourself! Be Christo-centric, rather than ego-centric!"

Sheila Cassidy: Key facts
Born 1937. Spent part of childhood on a farm in Australia. Educated at an Australian convent school, Sydney University and Oxford University. Deep religious conversion as a teenager. Trained as a doctor. Worked at hospitals in Oxford and Leicester. Went to Chile December 1971. Worked in hospitals and clinics there until 1975, including in a church-run clinic in a Santiago shanty-slum. November 1975 she gave medical treatment to a wounded revolutionary who was on the run from the secret police. This led to her arrest and torture. She spent 8 weeks in prison, three of them in solitary confinement. Her case aroused a storm of international protest; after pressure upon the Chile authorities by the British government, she was finally released and expelled from the country, arriving back in England December 30, 1975. Since then she has addressed many human rights' meetings; is now preparing herself for the religious life.